Never Get Lost Again

NAVIGATING YOUR HR CAREER

D0880396

Never Get Lost Again

NAVIGATING YOUR HR CAREER

NANCY E. GLUBE
PHYLLIS G. HARTMAN

Society for Human Resource Management
Alexandria, VA

The Society for Human Resource Management (SHRM) is the world's largest association devoted to human resource management. Representing more than 250,000 members in over 140 countries, the Society serves the needs of HR professionals and advances the interests of the HR profession. Founded in 1948, SHRM has more than 575 affiliated chapters within the United States and subsidiary offices in China and India. Visit SHRM Online at www.shrm.org http://www.shrm.org/.

Interior and Cover Design: Shirley E.M. Raybuck

Library of Congress Cataloging-in-Publication Data

Glube, Nancy E., 1947-
  Never get lost again : navigating your HR career / Nancy E. Glube and Phyllis G. Hartman.
       p. cm.
  Includes index.
  ISBN 978-1-58644-136-4
  1. Personnel management--Vocational guidance. I. Hartman, Phyllis G., 1949- II. Title.
  HF5549.G567 2009
  658.30023--dc22
                              2009011863

The Road Not Taken

Two roads diverged in a yellow wood,
And sorry I could not travel both
And be one traveler, long I stood
And looked down one as far as I could
To where it bent in the undergrowth;

Then took the other, as just as fair,
And having perhaps the better claim,
Because it was grassy and wanted wear;
Though as for that the passing there
Had worn them really about the same,

And both that morning equally lay
In leaves no step had trodden black.
Oh, I kept the first for another day!
Yet knowing how way leads on to way,
I doubted if I should ever come back.

I shall be telling this with a sigh
Somewhere ages and ages hence:
Two roads diverged in a wood, and I —
I took the one less traveled by,
And that has made all the difference.

— *Robert Frost*

Contents

# Acknowledgments

This book was a lifelong journey for the authors and a multi-year project in its development. We could not have accomplished this work without the support and participation of certain individuals. Some are quoted in the pages, and some helped with editing, formatting, and other book chores. Some are close allies, family, and friends who gave us moral support. To them, and any others we may have failed to mention, we say, "Thank you, and may your lifelong journeys be satisfying and safe."

We would like to thank the following people: Gail E. Aldrich, SPHR; Christopher Anzalone; Wendy Bliss; Linda Boatwright; Laura Buck, SPHR; Trenell Butler; Mary Knight Cherry; Judy Cheteyan; David Cochenour; Jim Dyak; Bryna Fireside; Jean Forti, Ph.D.; Denise Fenrick; Jessica Frincke; Steve Gray; Jack Greaf; James Hazen, Ph.D.; Keith Hicks; Bob Knight; Robert LaGow; Sharlyn Lauby, SPHR, CPLP; Joe Martucci; Pat Matthews; Ron McKinley, Ph.D.; Anne Miller; Anne-Margaret Olsson; Susan Post, SPHR; Chris Posti; Christine Reilly; Susan Renda, SPHR; Di Ann Sanchez, SPHR; Jennifer Schramm; Latricia Smith; Ommy Strauch, SPHR; Diane Tuccito; Sally Wade, SPHR; Beverly Widger, SPHR; and Nancy Woolever, SPHR.

Special recognition is appropriate for close family members who traveled with us during portions of our life journeys. In particular, the following family members offered technical support, spent hours listening and giving us feedback on ideas, and, in the case of our spouses, have been patient as we have "given birth" to this book. We would like to give our love and thanks to Howard Levenberg, Dana Levenberg, Karen Levenberg, Rachel Glube, Chuck Hartman, and Matt Hartman.

# Preface

We have been HR practitioners in corporate and consulting environments for a combined total of more than 50 years. We have enjoyed successful and satisfying careers in Human Resources and anticipate increasing our contribution to the HR community in the future.

As we have traveled our career road, we have worked in HR leadership roles in a variety of industries in the manufacturing and service sectors — in small, medium, and large companies in both the corporate world and consulting venues. In addition to contributing to the organizations of our employers and the communities they serve, we have often advised and counseled, hired and fired, planned, developed, and driven strategies for thousands of clients.

Throughout our careers, we have found ourselves educating, training, and influencing hundreds of HR professionals as they moved along their career paths.

Our commitment to Human Resources runs deep. While we've had meaningful career experiences and many successes, we've also made our share of mistakes. We've reached critical crossroads in our own careers in instances where we were unsure about which direction to turn: Should we stay with the mainstream or choose "The Road Not Taken" to quote the famous poem by Robert Frost? Throughout the course of our careers, we have traveled and will continue to travel many unknown roads.

In our own careers, we were able to receive good advice from people (coaches and mentors) in our respective networks. At times we wished we had more resources available that were targeted to the HR profession. We looked for a dedicated guide, a "one-stop shop" that would help us. But we didn't find one. For these reasons, we decided to create one by writing this book.

We came to realize that the HR "space" was unique. Career guidance and development have taken a different direction within the HR ranks, and there are considerable gaps. Prior to writing this book, we conducted market research and found career advice for the HR professional to be scarce. When we started to tell our colleagues that this book was under development, we received lots of encouragement, and we hope that you will find information that will help in your career journey.

Human Resources is becoming a highly regarded profession essential for business success. In addition, it has been defined with a specific set of competencies and knowledge. Today, HR certifications are widely sought, as they assure our business partners that we have a specific body of knowledge and skill.

We want to be travel guides for others in the profession as they move through their careers. Specifically, we want to pass along our own experiences and knowledge, as well as those of our colleagues.

This book does not reveal the latest scientific research on HR careers, nor is it an academic work. It is a practical travel guide, which aggregates advice, tips, and experiences from others. It presents success stories as HR professionals journeyed to their desired destinations. It recognizes roadblocks and barriers, and even considers how to deal with career derailment.

You may find that sections of this book offer information that you already know. If you realize that you do "know this stuff," our question to you would be: "Are you using what you know to manage your career?" We hope to put useful information and advice in your hands. The rest is up to you.

You may find parts of this book controversial, as we have confronted issues about the perception of Human Resources that has not always been positive. It is important to explore and, where possible, explain the root causes of these perceptions so you can develop methods to reverse them. Our purpose in considering these items is meant to be constructive and a basis for learning.

As you navigate your own career options, you'll find that building and maintaining personal relationships is critical. In addition to one-on-one contacts, you'll find that technology will be important in propelling your work forward by connecting you with resources and people.

Here are several notes to keep in mind as you read this career travel guide:
- We have strived to provide a book that is practical, approachable, and easy to read. We respect the busy professional lives of our readers.
- Chapters do not need to be read in order. Our intent is to provide a resource for readers to be able to pick up "here and there" during short time intervals, where information is easy to access and readily understood.
- We've included charts, checklists, illustrations, examples, and war stories to make it easy to use.

- The input of many people is found in our work. While the information from our various sources is factual, we have taken steps to protect the confidentiality of these sources as appropriate.
- Definitions:
    » "we" refers to the authors;
    » "associates" refers to nonmanagement employees; and
    » "clients" refers to the internal clients of organizations we serve.

The Shoemaker's Children Travel Barefoot

Kevin has been an entry-level HR generalist in a service organization for about three years. He enjoys what he is doing and has made a commitment to Human Resources as a career. While he enjoys his work, he senses differences between himself and his counterparts in other functional groups. Sometimes he feels a bit uncomfortable in their presence and senses the feeling might be mutual. Their departments seem to have more financial latitude and employees there seem to get ahead faster. Kevin is about to plan his next career step. What does he need to understand about the evolution of Human Resources in order to do this?

How Is Human Resources Different?

Professionals in sales, marketing, operations, IT, finance, and other corporate groups receive direction and guidance on how to steer their careers partly as a result of corporate programs, which are established by their employers and implemented by their supervisors and the HR professionals who service them. In addition to formal career development and mentoring programs, informal networks sprung up in their organizations that provided the rudder to keep their careers on course.

In many cases, these clients would reach out to us for advice as they hit certain career benchmarks or experienced career issues. In addition to responding to their requests, as dedicated HR professionals, we proactively monitored the careers of these individuals to ensure that they received the proper training and development, and consideration for promotions or other jobs which would advance their careers. We also ensured that they were well represented in terms of race and gender. When disappointments in their careers had to be faced, and when they didn't get the nod for a coveted position, we provided the safety net and the perspective to help them recover and continue to "fight the (career) fight."

However, while the HR professionals were cheerleading their clients on to greater heights, who was guiding Human Resources? This is not to say that HR functions conceptually don't want to groom and develop their own, or shouldn't take on the accountability to do so. While the motivation is there in many cases (under the best of circumstances), how often does it happen? As HR professionals, we are often so busy helping others — because that is our self-image and the perceived expectation — that our own careers often take a back seat.

This is the classic example of the shoemaker's children having no shoes. To explore the origins of this situation, how would you respond to the following questions?

- If organizations are going to look to Human Resources to provide career guidance and direction to their employees, shouldn't we "set the standard" by practicing it ourselves?
- How can we drive career development programs for others when our own house is not in order?
- If we do not practice these techniques for our own careers, are we providing the best advice and counsel to our clients?
- Does Human Resources deserve the same career focus as the clients it serves?
- Do the universal concerns about retaining the "best and the brightest" and building a career pipeline not apply to the HR community?
- Why is Human Resources an attraction for so many?

Mike D'Ambrose, senior vice president of Human Resources at Archer Daniels Midland, sums it up nicely:

> *The true gift of HR is its ability to inspire people to believe in themselves; to passionately seek the gold in every single person; and help each person find, develop and celebrate that gold. Every single person has something unique and wonderful to contribute. It is my job to ask our people, 'what are the things that you do great? How do we help you become this wonderful, unique contributor — not only to the company but also to yourself?'[1]*

The Evolution of Human Resources

The differences in perspective can be explained by examining the history of Human Resources and the psyche of the practitioners who serve in the field.

Deserving a Seat at the Table

Since the early 1990s, Human Resources has been coming into its own as a respected area of responsibility in the business world. Business leaders recognize that Human Resources' diligent attention to legal and regulatory compliance, implementation of talent assessment and development programs, focus on retention, and workforce planning are just a few of the contributions to the bottom line. In the contemporary environment of continuous organizational change as a result of reorganizations, downsizing, mergers, and acquisitions, Human Resources has earned its seat at the table because the value of human capital is being recognized. A "seat at the table" means that the HR role has been accepted as a key decision-maker for the organization along with all the other traditional functions in the organization. In the war for talent, Human Resources has made a real contribution as a differentiator between companies, especially when considering challenges around retaining key employees and engaging the rank and file. Specialists from a variety of fields are called in to negotiate difficult labor situations, to plan for offshore employment needs, and to understand and manage through cultural differences. HR professionals are moving on to assume opportunities in line positions because they are respected for their business knowledge and expertise.

The Value of Human Resources

A Challenging Evolution

Human Resources has not always garnered the respect it has today. Furthermore, in some scenarios, there are still "growing pains" to be worked out. Some companies still don't understand the value that Human Resources brings to the organization. Some independent business owners perceive Human Resources as a necessary evil, an administrative cost which causes them to give up the reins of power and presents roadblocks to how they want to manage their businesses.

Human Resources had typically been the "catch all" function for duties and individuals for whom you couldn't find a logical place in an organization. Typically, people who were placed in Human Resources had been unsuccessful in other roles, floundering in their careers, and may have had substandard performance. For example, one of the authors of this book assumed a Human

Resources Director role where the incumbent had been in the job for more than 20 years. The job was available because he retired. The retiree had first joined the company when Human Resources was starting to take shape as a profession. While we found the incumbent well liked and highly regarded by the employees, the department was in shambles. It turned out that the popularity he enjoyed was because he rarely took a stand. The few policies that existed were not enforced, and there was no accountability. They had an active relocation program at the time, but home appraisals were accepted from people with improper credentials. In some cases, the appraisals came from the relatives of the employees who were relocating! This situation was allowed to go on for years. When the president of the division assumed his role, he identified the problem issues and acted on changing out the incumbent. It took years for the new HR person to re-educate the employee population and rebuild the credibility of the HR function.

From Personnel to Human Resources

Even "Human Resources" is a relatively new term, replacing what used to be called "Personnel." "Human Resources" is now beginning to migrate to "Human Capital" or "Human Assets" or "Talent Management." Heads of Human Resources are now referred to as Chief People Officers (CPOs) or Chief Human Resources Officers (CHROs). Organizations have learned the value of Human Resources as the objective voice making financial, but, more importantly, strategic recommendations to the organizations they serve. HR departments have made progress in being able to quantify their accomplishments and show their value to the bottom line.

Successful organizations include the HR voice in the key decision-making process and have understood business set backs or reversals as a result of not doing so. Human Resources has grown to be the protector of an organization's legal risk.

Companies have had some tough HR lessons to learn. In the 1980s, Publix Supermarkets settled a multi-million-dollar lawsuit as a result of hiring inequities in their supervisory ranks. Nordstrom's department stores suffered litigation as a result of wage and hour violations pertaining to the overtime of their sales personnel. More recently, Microsoft was cited for improperly categorizing independent contractors and not putting these contractors on the payroll with benefits. These issues result in big headlines and big dollars, and companies have come to realize that Human Resources can help prevent them.

For some time, "Personnel" was a group charged with completing a set of loosely organized clerical functions that had to get done but were not viewed as strategically important. Other examples of classic "Personnel" functions include keeping logs of who came on or off the payroll, tabulating health insurance benefits enrollments and costs, planning company social events, and so on. These roles were largely held by female clerical workers, who tended to be detailed and responsive.

In many cases, "Personnel" was connected in some way to payroll functions and provided timekeeping or recordkeeping services. In some situations, "Personnel" was the same group of people who prepared the payroll. Later, when conflicts of interest were better understood between payroll and "Personnel," the payroll area was removed to operate separately, under different management. During this evolution, it was common for "Personnel" to report to a chief accountant, controller, or CFO. Executives who held the financial reins had the power to dictate to "Personnel" what to do and when. They held the reins to the budget expenditures, for example, and they often controlled health and welfare costs. If sales were down, and expenses were up, the finance or accounting department would tell "Personnel" that some sacrifices were needed. This was another way of calling for a decrease in headcount, or "downsizing," as it is called today. If the decisions were being made only on this basis of financial considerations, there was often a lack of objectivity and consistency. These decisions were often made in isolation, and often without consideration for their impact on other HR consequences (for example, on employee relations or retention).

Understanding the Past to Reinvent the Present

Why is understanding this evolution and history of Human Resources important to the role of Human Resources today? And how does it relate to the focus of a guidebook on the career development of HR practitioners? The answer is based on history: Human Resources comes with some baggage that needs to be understood before considering why HR folks have different development needs. Although now that Human Resources has largely earned the "seat at the table," not everyone understands the role Human Resources should be playing there. While Human Resources is highly engaged in the strategy and operations of the business enterprise, there is still some "catching up" to do.

Human Resources in a "Defensive" Posture

Despite its many contributions to the organization, HR professionals will always have to defend their position as a nonrevenue-generating body, as well as realize that they do not have the same clout as other business groups. We do want to give credit to those HR organizations that have developed profit centers through the sales and marketing of HR software products, training programs, earning tax credits, etc. We do note, however, that they are in the minority, take time to establish, and can divert attention away from the work of supporting the business.

While improvement can be noted around the "tail wagging the dog" and finance people dictating where cost cutting will come from on issues relating to human assets, in the face of a financial downturn in the organizations they service, HR resources and budgets have been and will likely continue to be the first to come under scrutiny.

In recent years, many organizations have outsourced routine HR functions previously performed in-house. Assuming these initiatives work properly and do cut costs, these steps have been helpful in shoring up Human Resources' credibility in the organization and earning respect for its business-like, bottom-line orientation. The other advantage is that making these moves has allowed the HR organization to focus on more strategic areas of the business where they provide higher value.

HR Orphans

While Human Resources has made considerable progress in developing clout and respect within the organization, all is not equal in the organizations they serve. We have experienced discussions where some kind of decision or consideration is made affecting all of the functions in the organization. It might be about making additions to the compensation plan or adding functionality to the Talent Management program. If it involves enhancements, more often than not Human Resources is overlooked in the discussion. If, on the other hand, it is about takeaways such as headcount cuts, then Human Resources is typically near the top of the list.

Also, how many times do our clients say, "You are HR. You are different"? While there may be a factual basis to this statement — because at times Human Resources does not fit the mold based on its unique role — the comment can be delivered in a negative way. In addition, when seen as keeper of the company policies and processes, Human Resources sometimes has been tagged as being the "police" or a "traffic cop." We can recall many instances where the conversation in the room would come to a halt when the HR contact enters.

Sometimes this "police label" is legitimate because, at times, we don't do a good job of "thinking out of the box." We tend to stick to the letter of the law rather than providing creative or new ways to apply a policy or work a business solution.

- What about the case of the star performer who has maxed out in the salary grade? Do we find a creative solution to retain him in the company or do we push back saying, "We've never done that before"?
- Then there is the unhappy client who can't find a suitable candidate for a critical position. While our budget does not allow for executive recruiters, do we find another way to source for the position?
- Finally, there is the case of the employee whose spouse is gravely ill, and, due to a computer glitch, has been denied insurance coverage. If the service center is closed for the day, do we tell him that tomorrow is another day, or do we pull out all the stops to make it happen today?

We can be rightfully accused of being risk-adverse and buried in the weeds instead of focusing more on strategy. In defense of the mid-level HR practitioner, they may not have the authority to loosely interpret policies or to apply untested solutions. However, they do have the ability to escalate or recommend to someone who does; they should look for opportunities where this "broker role" can be further developed.

Other Repercussions

Based on how the HR role can be perceived as "second-class citizen" status, sometimes there is additional negative fallout. Higher salaries, better benefits and other perks are often more generously applied to other departments, and Human Resources may not qualify. The irony is that the HR function has developed these programs to help the company stay profitable, competitive, and attract the top talent, and yet, at times, HR folks do not personally benefit. Typically, HR people do not get the same opportunities to socialize with vendors, key internal clients, and contacts as readily as their counterparts in other functions. If these opportunities become available, typically one needs to be on a senior level to leverage them. How often do HR folks get invited to the company golf match or company benefit event, where informal relationships and mentorships are developed that later become the springboards to higher-level jobs, salaries, and perks?

Double Standards?

Traditionally, HR groups are subject to tighter budget restrictions, less spending, and more stringent headcount levels. When business results head south, more belt-tightening occurs. HR professionals are continually expected to do more with less headcount while their counterparts in other functions are not likely to be as restricted. These conditions further impact the opportunity for career training and development activities. As headcount levels shrink, working hours become longer, and performance outputs/expectations increase. The direction is given that career training and development activities must be put aside for the moment. How often do we come back to them? How often is the energy there to go back and actively pursue them?

Challenges to Retention

Our investment in the grooming and development of HR practitioners may be called into question, as our better performers may grow impatient with the different "rules" and the slower career progression through the organization. They may seek different roles internally or externally as they eye the progress being made on career advancements by those they serve. They believe that — as HR professionals — they are not keeping pace. We recommend that HR professionals take an assignment in another part of the organization to round out their experience, to build their knowledge about the business, and to learn its language. After their experience there, we hope they come back. As transference in and out (to other functional areas) of Human Resources increases, there is more likelihood for a potential trend.

Time to Don Shoes

According to Matthew D. Breitfelder and Daisy Wademan Dowling, a career in Human Resources is the "next big thing." As stated in their white paper, *Why Did We Ever Go Into HR?*[2], Breitfelder and Dowling are recent Harvard MBAs who opted out of traditional careers in investment banking, general management, and business consulting to launch careers as HR practitioners.

These talented professionals feel strongly about the increasing importance Human Resources will play in future organizations. They say:

> But the staggering cost of finding and hiring top talent today — not to mention the millions of dollars' worth of productivity that can be left unrealized when a company's employees aren't engaged with their jobs — highlights the need to devote more time and resources to developing and managing this greatest asset. The stakes are becoming ever higher as the human-capital services sector continues to grow; as workers' mobility increases and moving laterally becomes more attractive to some people than moving up; as Baby Boomers vacate their corner offices, decreasing the supply of experienced managers; and as the Millennial generation brings new expectations to

the workplace. In short, the long-held notion that HR would become a truly strategic function is finally being realized.

In light of the increasingly important role of Human Resources, as well as its values, and challenges around acceptance and credibility, what do we need to do to groom our HR professionals to believe that they are important, attended to, and have the right to the same training and educational opportunities that their counterparts in other functions are receiving?

If the expectation is that Human Resources will carry the scepter of career learning and development for the entire organization, and if they are to appropriately and effectively drive initiatives around talent acquisition and succession, and if they are to evaluate and assess the talent of the corporation, and if we are entrusting the "care and feeding" of our precious human assets to them, then what can be more important than their own career training and development?

What Initial Steps Can I Take?

This book is meant to provide you with thoughts and ideas on how your "career journey" can be successful. As you plan for this lifelong trip, you might want to start by taking a snapshot of your current organization to see where it fits into the evolution of Human Resources.

Table 1.1 is a checklist for looking at your organization.

Table 1.1 Assessing Your Organization's HR Career Development Savvy

1. Does my current employer have a good reputation for HR practices?	Y	N
2. Does my current employer support HR career development?	Y	N
3. Does my current supervisor support HR career development?	Y	N
4. Do I understand how my current employer makes money?	Y	N
5. Do I understand the finances and business jargon of my company?	Y	N
6. Do I need additional education or training to reach my career goals?	Y	N
7. Am I committed to my own career development as an HR professional?	Y	N

The following chapters will examine these and other issues in more detail.

Final Thoughts

- The history of Human Resources gives perspective on challenges to our career development.
- Knowing our history can help us plan our future and avoid neglecting ourselves.
- Looking back helps us understand and better communicate with individuals, business leaders, and even peers who may not always see the value of our profession.
- Understanding our roots allows us to recognize the importance of taking the time and using the resources necessary to grow our careers.
- Knowledge allows us to examine organizations so that we can choose those that value Human Resources and support HR professionals' careers.

Travel Observations from the Experts: A 360-Degree View

Bill has been an HR generalist in a transportation company for 10 years. He has held several staff positions there. Recently, he has been thinking about expanding his horizons by moving to another company within one to two, years as there aren't many leadership opportunities in his current organization. He hasn't looked for another job in a decade and feels out of touch with what's going on "out there." He wants to get a better idea of what decision-makers value in HR professionals these days and what he needs to do to advance his career.

Some people are hesitant to ask for directions when they are traveling. They like to tough it out by themselves. They might view asking for directions as a sign of weakness. We all get so immersed in daily responsibilities that we fail to step back and determine if we are heading down the right road to achieve our career goals. We need to stop regularly to consult our travel itineraries, to analyze, and to check calibration. Asking for feedback is critical to operating on a strategic level. The "MO" of effective leaders is to regularly ask for feedback and to incorporate it into their personal operation plan.

Human Resources as a Critical Role for the Future

As mentioned in Chapter 1, Matthew D. Breitfelder and Daisy Wademan Dowling turned down "typical" careers in investment banking and strategic management to accept positions in Human Capital Management. To the consternation of associates and friends, they made a conscious decision to be in Human

Resources. Their argument is relevant to everyone considering or committed to Human Resources as a career: "HR today sits smack-dab in the middle of the most compelling competitive battleground in business where companies deploy and fight over the most valuable of resources — workforce talent."[1] They are committed to Human Resources for the long haul because they believe it has an important and challenging future:

> *This HR of the future has five characteristics. It, like a business school, promotes active learning; it serves as an engine for both savings and revenue; it hatches and harvests ideas across organizational boundaries; it makes big places smaller by connecting people intimately and often; and it focuses on the positive, moving beyond fixing problems and enforcing rules to enhancing employee engagement and capitalizing on people's strengths. If that's what HR is becoming, why wouldn't you go into it?*

The war for talent, the concerns about talent shortages, and their impact on the future viability of corporations has triggered some unusual moves in corporate America. In August of 2008, Kohl's department stores announced that CEO Larry Montgomery would be responsible for additional functions, including Human Resources. Moreover, the corporation promoted company president Kevin Mansell to CEO based on his strengths in talent management, which has been a strong suit for Kohl's. Both executives make more than $2 million in total compensation annually.

While some speculated that the moves were some kind of punishment or demotion for Montgomery, retail industry experts eschewed this sentiment and applauded Kohl's on having a well-thought-out succession plan. Jeffrey Cohn, a succession planning advisor said, "It's not unusual for a CEO to want to stay involved with a company's talent."[2]

Catch-Up Is Necessary

While the future of Human Resources is promising for those who are interested in strategic work or roles within the C-Suite, there are critics of Human Resources. Some criticism is a product of the roles Human Resources has fulfilled in its evolution (see Chapter 1). Others do not view HR professionals as business people because they lack the related knowledge and skills. While some internal clients have a dire need for the services Human Resources *should* provide, there is a level of frustration because their expectations have not been met.

A 2005 survey by the Hay Group provides examples of where Human Resources has fallen short.[3]

- 40 percent of employees complimented their companies for retaining high-quality workers;
- 41 percent said that performance evaluations are fair;
- 58 percent rated job training as favorable; and
- 50 percent of nonmanagers thought their companies took a real interest in their well being.

The majority said they had few opportunities for advancement and didn't know what was needed to move up.

Keith H. Hammonds has been critical of the HR profession, and you should take the time to read his article, "Why We Hate HR."[4] Whether you agree or disagree with the assessment, it offers a useful summary of common perception about Human Resources.

According to Hammonds, in a related article, Human Resources needs to explain things in the context of what the company believes; connect data to business indicators instead of activities; be knowledgeable about the business; and link HR with business strategy and goals. Human Resources also needs to represent management with integrity and honesty — and back employees in the name of improving the company's capability.[5]

Key Development Gaps

In light of the focus on key organizational issues, the role of strategic Human Resources will continue to evolve. Corporate assets will be less about equipment and more about people. As Human Resources continues to outsource routine payroll and administrative functions to "clear the decks" for more strategic work, HR practitioners will find their workday evolving into different roles. In order for Human Resources to excel in these areas, a skill and knowledge inventory must be conducted.

In October 2008, a group of senior HR leaders from the SHRM-Atlanta Chapter assembled to begin to create a curriculum for a SHRM Leadership Academy for the chapter. The Academy will offer training and development resources for high-potential HR professionals from companies that are members of the chapter. The curriculum will prepare attendees, who will be selected through a stringent application process, to assume strategic leadership positions in Human Resources.

Part of the preparation for this program included a list of important factors for professional development for Human Resources. We've created a checklist based on those factors (see Table 2.1). Rate yourself on your current expertise in each of these categories. Then show this list to someone who knows you well professionally, and ask them to rate you on the factors. Develop an action plan for each category where you need improvement. The comments from the *360° Travel Poll* (provided later in this chapter) may also be helpful to you in formulating the action plan.

Results of Our "360-Degree" Travel Poll

We interviewed HR practitioners and executives from a variety of industries and backgrounds in both corporate and consulting roles to get their impressions of Human Resources — including "the good, bad, and the ugly." They are our "Eyes and Ears" of the profession. Their comments are summarized below. It is important to note the common threads they talked about: truly understanding the business and its jargon, spending time working outside of Human Resources, and building relationships with business leaders on a daily basis. Each one provided practical tips, which should be considered when developing the action plan suggested earlier in this chapter.

Positive Perceptions

Steve Gray (VP, General Manager, ATT Mobility)

HR professionals are good enablers in the career advancement of people. Those who are most effective are able to achieve a great balance of the enabler side and the business side. They are able to keep their senior-level clients in check who strive the get the results "no matter what." They are able to stay in touch with what is going on with their clients in the business and not get isolated, especially in the case of large companies.

Diane Tuccito (Director, HR Solutions, Kinetix)

HR practitioners have been successful keeping companies out of trouble. They have a good understanding of the legalities that can impact the companies they serve. Based on their knowledge, they have credibility to advise their clients on potential risks. At their best, they are the leaders who drive the Code of Conduct or company policy. They can work with attorneys on employee relations cases looking for early resolution, keeping the opportunity for litigation to a

Table 2.1

Factors		Rate Yourself
Experience	• Assignment or job outside HR • Assignment leading others • Developing business acumen • Recipient of meaningful mentoring experience	
Characteristics	• Business toughness • Confidence • Maturity • Personal credibility • Able to jockey strategic and tactical situations • "Presence" in front of business leaders"(e.g., appearance, dress, communications style) • Able to align key business relationships • Creativity • Open to advice	
Skills	• Communication skills: verbal, written, persuasive, presentations • Able to coach • Able to offer realistic and sound counsel • Negotiation skills • Influencing in matrixed situations • Adaptability to change	
Knowledge	• Able to leverage technology • HR technical expertise on strategic issues, employment law, etc.	

minimum. Due to their panoramic view of the organization, they can keep tabs on remedies applied to treatment of employees and drive consistent application. Using a proactive approach, they can diffuse employee relations situations in the earliest stages. They can spot trends, educate clients, prevent recurrence, and contain the dollars that are spent on legal issues.

Jim Dyak (Principal, HR Dimensions, Inc.)

HR professionals are good listeners. They help influence the organization in the right direction. They have a seat at the table, but they also need to know what to do while they are sitting there. They need to know how to make a contribution to the business.

David Cochenour (VP, HR, InComm)

A lot of progress has been made in our profession in the last 10 years. We have been able to develop the concept of business partner and show value to the organizations we serve. However, the perception of Human Resources is case-specific and varies based on the organization. (David prides himself on understanding the business. He is an HR executive in the prepaid card industry, which has experienced double-digit growth in recent years. He told us about a situation where one of the officers he works with experienced a resignation on his staff, and there was a discussion about how to replace his services. David was able to speak about the business process that was impacted by the resignation, "wowing" his client. This kind of exchange is what we have to strive for in our relationships with our clients.)

Keith Hicks (Vice President, HR, Radiant Systems, Inc.)

The HR profession has come a long way in recent years. HR professionals understand people and what motivates them. They have been successful in getting teams to be most effective. They have been helpful in getting managers to be better leaders.

The HR people who have been the most successful achieve a perfect balance between business and people. If either end of the equation is less or more than 50 percent, the success quotient is compromised. This is a hard balance to achieve and maintain for the following reasons:

- Old habits die hard. Some HR professionals haven't had an appropriate role model to follow.
- HR professionals often avoid the business issues because they don't have the appropriate knowledge.

Areas for Improvement

(Gray)

They need to do a better job at developing a good business foundation. HR professionals are soft on Human Resources and business metrics. They don't spend time on metrics and don't see them as part of their role. They need to be conversant on the metrics as the engines that drive the business. Instead, they are more comfortable in a transactional role. Although HR functions have been outsourced to allow more time for strategic work, the shift has not happened yet.

(Tuccito)

At their worst, HR practitioners carry the policies to the extreme and are then perceived as the "police." They are viewed as rigid and unbending, which creates barriers between them and their clients. (Based on interviews the authors conducted, HR professionals need to use the policies as a guideline to create workable solutions that benefit their clients.) In addition to understanding the laws, they need to learn better application of them in a business setting. Instead of carrying a "big stick," they should be able to assess the subtleties of situations as a basis for working a solution that will fit expressly with the situation at hand and not a "cookie cutter" approach or not because "this is the process we have always followed." They should guide their clients about what can be done within a legal framework, what will make operations more efficient. HR professionals need to look at business issues more strategically and globally with a focus on what *can* be done.

(Dyak)

Often people end up in Human Resources by accident. While they like mingling with people and helping them, they are perceived as passive. They tend to sit in their offices waiting for someone to come in with a request or with an assignment. They need to learn to make the business case without clinging to a law or policy. CEO's can bristle at policies. The main thrust is to make the business case first. The law or policy should be presented as a side issue. With a better understanding of the business, they can position themselves to play a more assertive role.

(Cochenour)

Many HR types have not progressed past an administrative role. HR professionals must acquire the knowledge and skills to be the business person first and foremost. We need to strive to be business people first with a specialty in Human Resources. Too often the part about knowing the business, if it is present, gets tacked on at the end as a priority. HR professionals should learn the business skills through the compensation and benefits side of the business as these areas have great impact on the financials. Additional knowledge can be gained through formal and continuing education programs, mentoring, partnering with business leaders, and most importantly making this piece [a] priority.

They should be able to confidently participate in a conversation about the business on par to other functional leaders. For example, it may be about a new product line that is being created or an issue of capturing market share from a competitor.

(Hicks)

The typical HR person is bureaucratic, a policy pusher, and an administrative person who gets in the way of progress. They are good at quoting the relevant policy, knowing payroll procedures, and the HR files, but have not progressed beyond this point.

Understanding Needs of the Business

(Gray)

HR professionals need to tie their work to the true business initiatives. They should develop a performance scorecard for the business that is tied to the work that they do.

(Tuccito)

HR professionals need to understand more about the needs of the customer. One way to do this is to increase their understanding of the business and the financial parameters that make it go. Human Resources needs to make difficult decisions based on the facts. Those considering Human Resources for a career should be advised not to work in Human Resources because they "love" people. If they are executing their roles properly, HR professionals will have to make difficult and unpopular decisions affecting those they like, those who are perhaps doing a good job for the company but who have made a mistake or who have gone astray. Instead of simply responding to a customer need, they need to think about the long-term strategy and impact of their recommendations. For example, instead of merely coaching the client that a top performer needs to be fired due to a policy breach, what is the future impact to revenues of firing the top performer and hiring a replacement? How will the gap be narrowed, what steps need to be taken? If HR professionals are not comfortable in this kind of decision-making role, they need to reconsider the career choice they have made.

Human Resources needs to understand thought processes of the business leaders. They need to understand where revenue for a profitable business comes from, what creates value for the stockholders. They need a thorough understanding of business terms. They should identify standard HR metrics that are measured the same way in every corporation. For example, profit margins are calculated consistently. However, the cost of turnover is probably calculated differently based on each organization. When HR practitioners attempt to benchmark their metrics externally, often it is challenging or meaningless due to the differences in the calculations.

(Dyak)

HR practitioners need to understand how the company makes money. It is more than looking at a balance sheet. A balance sheet is a snapshot of a certain point in time. They really need to understand how the people perspective fits into the company's ability to make money. Human Resources needs to act like the best sports teams in their relentless quest for talent. Having a common understanding of the needs of the business, they would look at the business plan every quarter and flex based on the changes in the business. They can help build the company's reputation in the industry.

(Cochenour)

HR professionals need to pay attention to how they frame things with their clients. They need to speak to the tangible business side of issues first in order to demonstrate their knowledge of the impact. Often they make the mistake of talking about "soft angles" like morale, for example. This might be the right answer, but they need to frame it in business terms that the internal client will understand. In this case, how do the morale issues manifest themselves in business terms? Perhaps it is a turnover statistic, or lengthy time to fill a job due to company reputation issues.

(Hicks)

Contrary to popular thinking, the company's employees come first, not the customers. The employees are the engine of the business, and the engine needs to be tuned up before you run the car. The employees are then the catalyst to motivate the customers.

Recommendations for HR Professionals

(Gray)
- Spend time outside of the immediate confines of Human Resources to build credibility with your clients. A taskforce or a special assignment works great.
- Be proactive and identify the issue for the client instead of waiting for the client to come to you.
- Market yourself to be distinctive.
- Understand the competitive business landscape.

(Tuccito)
Insert yourself in high-level business meetings to understand [the] decision-making process of business leaders. Find out how the talent management process can impact company revenue, for example.
- Read books on business strategy.
- Enroll in MBA programs.
- Find a business mentor or get exposure to high-level executives.
- Understand financial, sales, logistical, and technology components of company operations.

(Dyak)
- HR professionals should spend time with operating people to find out where their triggers are. Human Resources can show value by coaching their business partners to get them to correlate people assets to the bottom line using business case examples.
- HR practitioners are unable to "sharpen the saw" for themselves. They need to understand that they can cut more wood with a sharp saw. Being too busy is not a good excuse.
- Consider the value of professional certifications, which build credibility. Members of the C-Suite are starting to see the value of certifications in that they demonstrate that the holder has [a] grasp of a body of knowledge, shows motivation, and recognizes the need for continuous improvement. There are a growing number of clients who will not consider HR candidates for open jobs unless the candidates are certified.

(Cochenour)
Cochenour cites his own career development as helpful in getting him where he is today. He graduated in the 1980s and was able to land a general management

role after college, which offered him great training and orientation to the world of business. After that, he went on to assume a regional personnel position. He advises the following:

- Get broad exposure to the business by landing a job with a "brand name" quality company early in your career to gain credibility. Working in smaller companies is a better route after that.
- Do a stint in operations or finance during your career. It doesn't have to be a full-time job but can be a special project or initiative. By doing this you are building credibility as a business partner.
- Despite the long hours most HR professionals work, develop and maintain an active network along with mentors, coaches, or advisors. The people you build these relationships with are the same people who may be in the position to hire you at different points in your career.
- HR people turn out some of the worst resumes. The content looks like a list of activities or a job description. It is another indication that they don't see themselves in business terms. (See Chapter 9 for advice on writing effective resumes.)

(Hicks)

Hicks was a successful technology consultant for seven years. He was always interested in the people aspect of his role, i.e. hiring, development, etc. At one point, an opportunity came up for a HR leader, and he was interested. Although there was some speculation about whether his motive was to reduce his business travel load, this was not the case. Hicks took the assignment and has continued in Human Resources for nearly two decades. During this time, when he needed to fill open positions, he selected people who were in a business role with a predilection for Human Resources.

The biggest "ah ha" for Hicks was when he realized the amount of impact he could have on the business that he didn't have in his former role. His satisfaction in Human Resources stems from his commitment and ability to create a workplace environment where people can flourish.

He offers the following tips:

- Ask for a line assignment in the business as part of your career plan. Bring it up in the course of your career discussions with your manager. Explain that you believe such an assignment is an important part of your development to give you increased credibility with your clients. Be on the lookout for jobs in other parts of the company that interest you. If it is not a full-time job, it may be a role on a committee or task force.

- HR professionals are well regarded when their clients say, "They get it" and, "They understand my business and people. They are an advocate and support for me."
- Talk to leaders and other colleagues in the company on a proactive basis. Seek them out for lunch or for coffee to have discussions with them about the business on a weekly basis.
- Encourage your management to include knowledge of the business to be part of your job description if it is not there already. Take courses in finance and accounting to learn the basics. There are many opportunities to acquire this knowledge online without a cost. If possible, pursue a MBA.
- Learn the history of the business from the veterans or founders. Knowing the history will give you the context for why certain decisions are made. (For example, in one of the companies Hicks worked for, there was a widespread practice of offering stock options to everyone in the company regardless of their rank. At that time, the company was privately held and therefore the company had significant latitude in awarding options. When, later, the company went public, the practices related to options significantly changed. They became quite restrictive. The change caused an employee relations issue. Hicks needed to come up with another way to improve employee satisfaction. Without knowledge of the company history on stock options, he would not have had a clear understanding on the evolution of this issue.)
- Shadow your business partners as they perform their jobs. Attend a sales call or a planning meeting. Not only will these experiences improve your knowledge of the business, but they will also greatly increase the respect your clients have for you.
- Ask for feedback on a regular basis. Most HR professionals are not in the habit of doing this. When you finish an assignment, ask "How did I do?", "How can I do better next time?" Instead of just asking people who you know are your fans, also ask those all around you to get a complete view. Give them an objective source to transmit the information to in order to allow for anonymity. If necessary, ask a trusted colleague to collect the information for you. If you have the opportunity, a 360-degree feedback instrument is the best way to get input on key contacts catalogued and fed to you on a confidential basis. Once you get the feedback, be sure to act on it. Otherwise the effort is, at best, a waste of time; at worse, an erosion of your credibility.

Jack Greaf, CEO of Mitsubishi Electric Power Products, sees the HR professionals in his company as the glue that holds the organization together. To be strong glue they have to have a strong understanding of the tempo of the company and the industry they serve. HR leaders must be honest and fair, and at the same time able to balance the needs of the company and the employees. HR professionals must be business leaders. They need to lead by example.

 ## Final Thoughts

- Business expertise once viewed as a frill in Human Resources is now a necessity.
- Without the business orientation and two-way lines of communication about it, we won't make any progress on the hard-core HR issues.
- CEOs may see Human Resources as a roadblock to business success.
- We need to understand how others view Human Resources so we can work to reinforce the positive views and change the negative ones.
- Repeated messages from interviewed professionals include:
  » Learn how to express things in language that business leaders understand.
  » Be open to new ideas and suggestions.
  » Be willing to determine how the policies and rules can be created that help business succeed.
  » Recognize the true power that an influential HR professional can have in creating a successful business where both the organization and the people flourish.
  » Work for opportunities to experience other areas of the business outside of Human Resources.
  » Follow the sage railroad crossing advice: Stop, Look, and Listen.
    - Stop doing Human Resources just for Human Resource's sake but rather connect everything you do to the business.
    - Look for opportunities to grow in business knowledge that can be applied to the HR functions.
    - Listen to ideas and thoughts from employees, business partners, customers, and suppliers to determine how to successfully conduct Human Resources.

- In economic downturns, everyone's position is precarious. Career planning must involve strengthening your hand to survive the threats to your organization.
- This is best accomplished by increasing your broad value to the organization.

Navigating a
Destination

Bob has been working as a recruiter in a large retail firm for about five years. He has a bachelor's in Business with a concentration in Human Resources. In school, he did learn some of the basic HR functions but discovered upon graduation that recruiting was the best available job in his area. He would like to branch out into some other HR area, maybe even into a top-level management job someday. He's met the CHRO and sees her as a great role model. He's also interested in helping to manage the recruiting function, since the company has a relatively high turnover rate. But he's not sure what kinds of jobs there are in Human Resources. He's ready to move forward in his HR career trip but first he has to decide where he wants to go.

Before you can move forward on your HR career journey, you need to have some short- and long-term goals about where you might want to go.

Thirty-eight percent of HR professionals got their current jobs through internal promotions, according to a recent survey.[1]

Looking for Trends

Some trends that may lead to "new" HR jobs are listed here. But we don't have a crystal ball, and we do recognize that change is constant and unpredictable. As you move forward in planning your next step on the career journey, we suggest that you read business publications regularly, such as the *Wall Street Journal*, and local business publications. Regularly search and read blogs and web sites that explore future trends. Maintain networks that go beyond your specific industry and Human Resources, and talk to those people about what they see coming down the road. Talk to people who are in recruiting, even if that is your area, since they often see where the talent pool is and what talent may be needed in the future. And join business organizations and professional associations (both local and national) that research future trends.

So where did you start and where can you go in your HR career?

It is critical that you engage in solid "strategic planning" for your career by looking at future projections for Human Resources and the workplace environment.

Pathways for the future may be different than those of the past, but the tips and techniques of those who have blazed the trails before us can give hints as to methods that will work for you in the future.

This chapter provides information on jobs that may be found within the HR function, as well as those outside of the function. It also explores the options for any HR professional to take their talents to other areas in the organization up to and including the CEO position. Finally, it provides feedback from a number of HR professionals outlining the paths they took to get to their present positions.

HR Careers

In today's organizations, HR jobs may vary but they tend to be divided into several general categories.

Generalist

Generalists are individuals who have broad HR knowledge and expertise, and perform more than two primary HR functions on a regular basis. A generalist may be positioned at many levels in an organization, since, in one sense, the Chief Human Resource Officer (CHRO), vice president of Human Resources, director of Human Resources, or the HR manager may be considered a generalist. The title of generalist, however, usually covers a lower-level professional position in a larger organization.

In a small organization, a generalist may be the only HR-functional job but may not even have an HR title. Titles for positions that may include generalist work can vary widely but may include HR administrator, HR associate, or HR assistant.

Specialist

Specialists usually focus on one functional area of Human Resources. Sometimes a specialist may lead in a specific function while supporting or working with other functions or a total HR team.

Again, there can be a number of titles associated with the specialist job. A vice president, director, manager, or associate can "unofficially" be a specialist in a particular functional area.

Specialist jobs are most likely found in larger organizations where there may be a need for a breakdown of Human Resources due to the complexity of the organization. In addition, large organizations that have a centralized structure may have specialists at the corporate headquarters level who deal with particular functional needs and support generalists in the field.

Specialization is also driven by the nature, culture and life stage of the business. For example, the U.S. automotive industry (facing serious global competition and dominated by labor unions) may need specialists in labor relations. A public-sector organization may need staffing specialists due to the impact of a changing political climate, which makes retention and recruitment an issue.

Table 3.1 gives some information on specialist jobs, what is done in those jobs, and, finally, some of the common metrics used to evaluate the success of that function.

There are times in which a combination of specialties comprises a job. For instance, in smaller organizations it is not unusual to see the combination of compensation and benefits functions since both relate to rewarding employees. Another common example is staffing and employee relations, since the individual doing the hiring may be seen as someone to whom the employees feel comfortable bringing their questions, issues, and challenges.

At other times, specialties are combined because of the skills and strengths that they require. For example, specialties that include working with numbers, working directly with people, or with writing skills might be combined. The other rationale for combining specialties is to better serve the needs of the organization's culture or unique environment or business.

Table 3.1 **Common Specialist HR Areas**

Function	Description	Key Metrics
Staffing (sometimes called Talent Acquisition) has become more prestigious due to growing talent shortages faced by organizations.	• Sourcing, recruiting, and hiring • Developing staffing plans, researching sources of candidates • Developing a knowledge of the work of the organization, as well as the culture • Maintaining up-to-date knowledge of legal issues • Training managers on interviewing techniques • Managing recordkeeping – may include EEO	• Turnover rates • Return on Investment (ROI) on sourcing methods • Yield ratio • Time-to-hire • Number of EEO complaints • Turnover costs • Vacancy rates and costs
Compensation – focus is on pay, but not just payroll issues. May be combined with benefits as the cost of "total compensation" becomes important.	• Salary budgeting • Establishing and maintaining compensation strategies, processes, and plans • Management relocation programs	• Compensation as a percentage of sales • Human Capital ROI • Human Capital Value Added • Pay rates comparison with industry standard and markets • Global pay comparisons
Benefits – includes insurance benefits, government-mandated benefits, work-life programs, flexible workplace issues, wellness programs	• Establishing strategies • Evaluating cost effectiveness and value of programs • Negotiating with outside benefit providers • Communicating benefits to employees and management • Ensuring legal compliance	• Employee usage • Cost per employee • Industry comparisons • Percentage of total compensation

continued on next page

Table 3.1 **Common Specialist HR Areas (continued)**

Employee Relations – includes dealing with day-to-day employee problems and trends and issues, as well as organized labor (unions).	• Primary employee contact for issues • Developing HR policies, practices, and employee handbooks • Coaching supervisors and managers on handling employee issues • Training employees re: policies • Day-to-day resolution of union problems, union communication, and grievances • Planning and carrying out union negotiations • Keeping a good relationship between the company and the employees, including union-avoidance campaigns • Dealings with labor attorneys (a law degree may be helpful)	• Number of cases in litigation • Number of settled out of court • Number of grievances and arbitrations • Turnover rates • Number of formal complaints
Risk Management – focuses on reducing the potential for losses by ensuring the employees have a safe and secure environment. May include ethics issues.	• Developing and managing safety programs • Security plans and policies • Keeping up with legal requirements, including OSHA regulations • Managing general liability and workers' compensation • Establishing policies and practices related to workplace ethics • Overseeing or managing Sarbanes-Oxley (SOX) Act compliance	• Injury rates • OSHA rulings • Comparison with industry rates • Number and severity of workers' compensation filings • Safety audit results • Insurance rates • Law suits and awards

continued on next page

Table 3.1 **Common Specialist HR Areas (continued)**

Human Resource Development (HRD) – deals with talent management and performance issues.	• Managing training programs • Developing employees • Developing, implementing, and evaluating activities and programs that improve the bench strength of the leadership team • Talent assessment • Succession planning	• Training ROI • Training investment factor • Turnover rates for key talent
Organization Development (OD) – more recently recognition as a competency necessary for strategically focused HR.	• Looking at the total organization and culture • Considering and planning for change • Promoting adaptive learning and knowledge management essential for organizational growth • Focusing on how to encourage creativity and innovation • Employee engagement is sometimes a subset of this area • Focusing on the way things happen and how an intervention can affect the necessary changes • Sometimes part of the HRD specialty	• Human Capital ROI • Human Capital Value Added

continued on next page

Table 3.1 **Common Specialist HR Areas (continued)**

Global Human Resources – this newer specialty area includes all of the generalist functions but with a broader look at how HR management works on a world stage.	• International Assignment Management: preparing employees for work in other countries • Integrating home country employees • Managing legal issues and coordination of policies and sometimes conflicting laws across the world • Specifying employees to assume overseas assignments • Developing an understanding of other cultures • Expatriating and repatriating employees • Working with home country nationals and third country nationals	• Success ratios for expatriates, including turnover rates • Number of legal issues • Profit margin comparisons for various country facilities
Diversity – this specialty has struggled with defining itself since it evolved from looking at Affirmative Action and EEO issues to a much broader consideration of the relationships and acceptance of all people in an organization.	• Creating a work environment or culture that allowed everyone to contribute • Enhancing the ability of people from different backgrounds to work effectively together • Leveraging differences and similarities in the workforce for the strategic advantage of the organization • Eliminating (or minimizing) prejudice	• Ratios of different groups represented in the workforce • Number of issues, grievances, etc., related to diversity • Number of EEO claims

Follow the Trends!

It's always risky to predict the future; however, there are some trends that may lead to new areas of responsibility for Human Resources.

Retention

Some companies may need to retain the intellectual capital of retiring Baby Boomers and at the same time attract and retain Millennials (Gen Y). Both of these groups appear to want flexibility and work-life balance in addition to customized reward structures. As a result Retention Specialists might be a career in these companies. This specialty may develop from a combination of employee relations and benefits that would focus on evaluating and providing flexible jobs and customized rewards. The retention specialist may also focus on getting these diverse groups to work collaboratively for the best interests of the organization.

Sustainability

The focus on green companies and sustainability, managing use of resources, and global warming at the writing of this book support the argument that Human Resources should be a major player as organizations establish sustainability initiatives.

Sustainability is viewed through several lenses, but at the least it involves a change in the behaviors of employees, which involves Human Resources. Human Resources may even share the lead role of "sustainability officer."

Corporate Social Responsibility

Adrienne Fox, in an article in *HR Magazine*, presented a focus on the need for business leaders to be involved in corporate social responsibility (CSR).[2] CSR includes ethical behaviors, contributing to the community development, and green or sustainability issues. This could result in an HR job as a CSR officer or a specialty that focuses on all of the components, i.e. transparent measures, values, global balance, etc.

Workforce Development

Concerns about the quality of literacy in students graduating from high school, as well two- and four-year colleges, was evident in a 2007 survey of businesses.[3] In addition, the concerns about a lack of qualified workers in fields that are facing increased retirements of boomers may require organizations to consider retraining and development of populations like the disabled and chronically unemployed individual to fill the gaps. These trends could lead to an HR specialty that focuses on workforce development working with schools and social service agencies. This specialty would be an expansion of the Human Resource development function.

HR Jobs Outside of an Organization

Jobs in Human Resources are not limited to working within an organization as an employee providing HR services to a group of employees. You might find more satisfaction or even more opportunities doing Human Resources as a consultant, an educator, an HR tools and systems vendor, or by using your HR expertise in other jobs in the organization.

Consultant. Some organizations refer to their internal HR professionals as "business consultants." This promotes the view of Human Resources as a business partner that offers specialized support, services, and advice to other functions or departments. That is not the definition considered here.

According to a 2007 survey by Watson Wyatt, HR functions are increasingly being outsourced to HR consultants.[4] The report indicated that 75 percent of companies surveyed outsource defined-contribution retirement plans, while 4 percent outsource performance management. Much of the growth in outsourcing is in more administrative aspects of Human Resources as companies make Human Resources more strategically focused. There is also an attempt to control costs using outsourced HR professional services on an as-needed basis, allowing them to keep the overhead associated with having in-house professionals limited. HR consultants may be individual practitioners who establish their own business. Consultants may also join other Human Resources or general consultants in a firm. A consultant may be a generalist who provides a range of HR functions and services, and advice to clients.

Generalist/Business Partner Consultants. Generalist consultants usually focus on a particular market or client base. Some deal with small- to mid-sized clients who need HR services but can't afford to have full-time HR employees. Others focus on large companies that wish to outsource some functions so they can focus internal Human Resources on more strategic issues. Some consultants work in a particular industry such as manufacturing, health care, or service since companies use consultants for their expertise and it may be difficult to be an expert in all industries. Geography may also play a part in who the consultant serves.

Some consultants work as sole proprietors and others may incorporate their businesses. The choice here depends on how big they expect the business to grow and how they cover any risk resulting from the business. As a consultant, the HR professional may give advice or provide services that cause the client to be sued or to loose money (even if it is good advice or service). As an "outsider," consultants typically protect their personal assets by filing for incorporation and/or getting liability insurance.

Specialist Consultants. Much like internal specialists, consultants may specialize in a particular HR function such as compensation, benefits, or recruiting. Often, specialists focus on those areas that can be more easily outsourced by organizations.

Other Consulting Firms. Consultant jobs can also be found within other consulting firms. For example, a CPA firm may have an HR consultant on its staff to provide advice and services for clients who may be too small to have an internal HR position.

Consulting may be done as an employee in a large HR-consulting firm or by buying a franchise in a particular area. Franchises are more common in the professional recruiting or outplacement industries.

HR Sales and Marketing. HR professionals who have an interest and an aptitude in sales and/or marketing may find positions in HR-service companies. Obviously, a good understanding of what Human Resources is all about would be a significant help in selling HR services. HR education and demonstrated experience gives a sales professional a certain level of instant credibility when they talk to HR customers or business professionals.

Educator. By 2014, the need for college professors will increase by 32 percent over the number of active college professors in 2004, says the U.S. Bureau of Labor Statistics.[5]

Though they take many forms, HR degrees seem to be becoming more prevalent. For example, there may be specific HR undergraduate and graduate degrees, or Human Resources may be a specialization in a Business degree program.

Due to the growth in these programs, there are likely to be more jobs available for HR educators. Often, a Ph.D. is needed for full-time tenure track positions. However, with a decline in individuals seeking their Ph.D. and more educational institutions trying to attract working, professional, adult students who want educators with real-life experience, there may be more openings for people with experience vs. education.

There are also opportunities for adjunct instructors in HR programs. Usually, a master's degree in Human Resources or significant experience is the minimum requirement of adjuncts.

The adjunct educator job is something that can be a supplement to a consultant's business. It can also be a good networking tool for HR recruiters in large companies, and can provide a possible retirement career path. The advantages of teaching include keeping up-to-date with current trends; meeting potential employees, vendors, employers, or clients; practicing your communication and presentation skills; and learning about what's going on in business through class research and discussions.

Suppliers and Vendors. Suppliers to the HR field may also be considered HR professional consultants when they are doing the actual HR work. In some cases, however, suppliers of services to Human Resources fulfill a specialty job that is not a typical HR function.

While suppliers may provide services in many HR functions, two examples are legal and data management areas.

Legal professionals may have started careers in Human Resources and then moved into providing services for companies in labor law. They can perform a wide range of tasks — from policy development and handbooks to investigations and compliance audits (after getting additional education, that is). In some cases, the organization's counsel may serve as an HR consultant.

Data management professionals in Human Resources include companies and individuals who process payroll and manage HRIS system conversions, as well as those involved with daily HRIS maintenance, providing Affirmative Action, and other software and support services.

General Business Management. The final pathway for Human Resources is as a part of the general business management. Some have said that any good people manager is a good HR manager. Having a solid HR background might be a passport to many other destinations in the organization.

In particular, HR professionals have moved into operations, administration, sales, and management positions by combining their HR knowledge with some additional education and/or experience. One of the authors had an HR business partner reporting to her who earned an MBA degree and successfully migrated to a role in sales operations. General business management is a legitimate path, especially in those organizations that provide services, since service depends upon people.

Once they develop HR expertise, HR professionals who started their careers in some other profession may be able to make the transition back to that field at a higher level.

The ultimate general business management job is, of course, the CEO, COO, or president. This path is still less common, but the numbers are increasing. The reality of talent management as the key to global competition makes filling these senior positions with people who have HR background more likely.

Follow the Leader

The following is a collection of paths a variety of HR professionals have followed to get to various jobs. While not intended to be specific directions, they provide some perspectives. Some of these individuals started their careers prior to the availability of specific HR degree programs and, in some cases, before there was a broad recognition of Human Resources as a career. These HR professionals may have started their careers from different directions but a pattern of specific HR education, an initiative to take advantage of opportunities to grow through experience, and the support of mentors and advocates are themes which are common throughout.

Focus on your talents, personality, interests, skills, and current knowledge. By adding competencies, skills, and the knowledge needed for your target job, you will be more likely to succeed.

From Bank Teller to HR Manager to CEO

Judy Cheteyan, PHR, president of ABDI, a distribution firm, started her work life as a bank teller at a time when the HR profession was seen as Personnel. Once she learned the job, she decided that her mission would be to "make every customer smile." This positive customer service attitude caught the attention of the bank manager who started her on the path to an HR job. It took an assertive effort to eventually get to associate HR manager, when she told management they needed her when they were having high turnover. The job also had little advancement opportunity. She recognized the need for formal education and pursued a certificate program at the University of Pittsburgh. Judy left the bank to take a job at the Society of Automotive Engineers (SAE), where she became the HR manager as the organization grew from a small staff that had been relocated from New York City to an organization of more than 350 employees. Having developed her leadership skills as the organization grew, she was promoted to a vice-president level. She left SAE to lead the smaller ABDI, where she says she uses her HR business knowledge every day.

Military Position Leads to HR Management

Ron McKinley, SPHR, started his more than 30 years in Human Resources in the military, where he assumed an operations and training role. Upon leaving the military, Ron continued in the training function in the private sector. His career advancement was a combination of continuing education — a bachelor's in Management, an MBA in Human Resources, and a Ph.D. in Administration and Management (Organizational Development).

Taking advantage of opportunities to get experience in a variety of Human Resources and business roles also helped Ron's advancement. He was a general manager in the Marriott Corporation, where he was recognized for his ability to develop new managers, a critical skill for someone in the training function. His Marriott division was responsible for 600 quick-service restaurants, and he served as the manager of Management Development.

After a few years, he realized that he wanted to learn more about other areas of Human Resources. Ron left Marriott to take a position in a smaller food-service company, Tico Taco, where he managed all of the HR functions for four years. He next worked for Long John Silver's for six years, starting as division HR director and achieving three promotions in five years to become the vice president of Human Resources.

Through a series of moves working in a customer service and sales company where he lead a 50-person HR staff and a strategic HR initiative in a highly competitive industry, as well as working as a senior HR consultant in a consulting firm, he honed his HR skills — using each step as part of his plan to get into senior management in a large organization. As vice president of Human Resources for Cincinnati Children's Hospital Medical Center, he heads Human Resources for one of the top two children's research hospitals in the United States. He manages an annual budget of more than $100 million and is a member of the President's Cabinet (executive leadership team). Ron credits his career success to his personal career strategic plan.

Political Science to HR VP to Consulting

After receiving her political science degree, DiAnn Sanchez, SPHR, thought she wanted to become a lawyer. However, some HR courses she took helped her realize that she "had to do HR." Her first HR job — for Kraft Foods as an HR generalist — provided her with the first of a series of great mentors who asked her what she wanted to do. Her answer, "I want to be a female, Hispanic executive." Her mentor told her she would need to work hard and learn about the business, including working in the plant with the employees.

Having a clear goal and working with her career mentors, she sought opportunities and took risks making strategic job moves working for Coca Cola, Pepsi, Dallas Fort Worth International Airport, United Natural Foods, the Boeing Commercial Airplane Group, American Airlines, and Delta Technology, a subsidiary of Delta Air Lines. In each job, she focused on learning the vision, mission, values, and business of the organization.

She followed the advice of one of her mentors to "make sure you have business partners that love you." She strived to develop all the aspects of Human Resources, as well as her strategic management skills. While still in her 20s, she had achieved executive management jobs and a master's degree in Organizational Management. With 25 years in a wide range of HR management positions, DiAnn founded DAS Consulting in 2008, to continue her love of learning about different businesses and discovering how to help them succeed.

Business Management, HRIS, and Union Experience Lead to Executive Level

With her business degree, Sally K. Wade, SPHR, started out as an executive secretary in a large manufacturing company. Rather quickly, she received an atypical promotion to assistant supervisor for a "steno" group of a dozen-and-a-half women. She got her first HR position as a compensation analyst. The head of Human Resources liked to mentor new professionals and tapped her to get involved with development of an HRIS system. When the project manager left to join IBM, Sally was asked to take the job.

At age 29 and a woman (it was unusual at that time for a woman to be in her employment position), she was responsible for purchasing and implementing the software. She reported to the vice president of Human Resources. Her organizational skills and the fact that they trusted her were significant factors. She moved up to HRIS manager and stayed with the company for more than a dozen years until the business climate changed and the company was forced to downsize. During this period, she was made manager of the Career Transition Center, finally laying herself off. Sally completed her master's in Business through the Transition Center.

Hired by Duquesne Light, a utility company to help install an HRIS system, she accepted the position with the request to move into a more generalist role when the project was completed. Her manager stayed true to her word and Sally worked for 10 years at Duquesne, reaching assistant vice president and corporate officer. She left the company during major restructuring as a result of deregulation. She took a position with a small manufacturing company as its vice president of Human Resources. Her next move was to a larger company, Mitsubishi Electric Power Products, Inc., where she became only the second woman to reach a vice-president level in Human Resources in the company's history.

Final Thoughts

- The HR profession takes many forms — don't limit your plans and thoughts.
- HR professionals may work within one organization or as consultants who work with many organizations.
- You can use your HR skills outside of Human Resources and you can "come home again."
- Look at the work involved in any career path and consider the necessary skills, competencies, etc.
- Be creative and consider how you can use you knowledge of the business to connect with your HR career path.
- At different times in your life, different paths may be better for you.

Mapping Your Route

Robbie is a workforce analyst in a large company. After completing his degree in Business, he has been in his role for a few years. Robbie was placed in this role due to his strong background in statistics. He has had an opportunity to work with some colleagues who head up the various HR functions, and it has inspired him to consider whether a career in mainstream Human Resources may be a good option for him. His manager is happy to help and has asked for more information about his interests, but, frankly, Robbie doesn't know where to start.

What were the circumstances that led to your position within Human Resources? Did you choose to be in Human Resources or did you end up there purely by chance? Perhaps you formerly worked in another functional area of the business, and it is part of a rotation for a career in general management, or maybe you volunteered to see what it is all about. Based on a 2008 survey, approximately 35 percent of HR professionals did not start their careers in the HR Department.[1] In the survey, 75 percent of the respondents were over the age of 35 when they started their careers. For this age bracket, Human Resources Management was not as fully recognized as a profession in many industries.

If Human Resources was part of your career plan, congratulations! You have apparently created a planning process that worked for you. Whether your goal is to continue working in Human Resources or to migrate to a different field, steps outlined in this chapter will help you leverage the planning process that was successful for you before.

If you ended up in Human Resources "by accident," you probably have some more work to do depending on your overall experience level.

As the field of Human Resources continues to evolve, a more deliberate approach will be needed. Human Resources is now perceived as a profession requiring a specific set of knowledge and skills in order to succeed. For instance, individuals who hold a CPA designation have a consistent and predictable knowledge base. Employers are seeking HR professionals holding certifications because it gives employers more confidence about what certification holders know and can do. An informal review of recent job postings for professional HR positions shows an increasing number preferring or requiring certification. It is really a form of quality assurance.

An unplanned landing in Human Resources may require backtracking to get a well-rounded HR education. You need to learn the HR roles, the relevant federal, state, and local laws and regulations, technical knowledge, and policies related to each of the functional areas, and an on the job "crash course" of how to actually handle a variety of employee relations situations. You will have more reading, shadowing, and training to do. Also, you will need to learn the terminology and jargon of Human Resources, which can be gained through formal professional development and education programs. The solutions to most real-world situations are not (and cannot be) learned in a textbook; they have to be experienced firsthand. As the HR profession has evolved, there are an increasing number of cases where a job opportunity in Human Resources is planned, and the related education and knowledge are HR-centric. As the field has grown and advanced, gaining entry to a HR career has become more competitive and will require more deliberate preparation and education.

Here's an example of a serendipitous "move" to Human Resources. One of the authors was a Spanish teacher in New York City during the 1970s and faced a career change as a result of a divorce and additional financial responsibilities for a young child. She decided to leverage her Spanish skills to get a job in the business sector despite her lack of business experience. She was able to land a job with a toy manufacturing company in the South Bronx, where Spanish was the native language of 90 percent of the local workforce. The company wanted to develop a Spanish language program for its first-line supervisors. They were looking for someone to direct this initiative as well as perform the duties of an entry-level HR staff position. This job was the beginning of a three decade (and counting) career in Human Resources.

Assuming that the readers of this book are already in the HR profession, what steps are you going to take to shape your future? Perhaps some travel plans are in order.

What Are the Prospects for Careers In Human Resources?

The prospect for jobs in Human Resources are excellent. Susan Healthfield, in her article, "So You Want a Career in Human Resources," said that many people are eager to start a career in Human Resources. Human Resources is a fast-growing career filled with many lucrative opportunities, according to Healthfield. She believes that career analysts expect the number of HR jobs to increase in the future. In addition, the median annual income for careers in Human Resources is above the national average.[2]

Companies have realized the value that Human Resources brings "to the table" and want the benefit it brings to their companies. However, keep in mind that, like any other field, there will be ups and downs based on supply and demand, and what particular field of expertise is running hot at the moment. For example, currently, with the expected exodus of Baby Boomers from the workforce, companies are looking for expertise in staffing and talent acquisition to establish strategies to backfill existing talent in a proactive way.

How Effective Are HR Practitioners at Career Planning?

Based on anecdotal information collected by the authors, more than 50 percent of the practitioners we spoke to admit that career planning is neither a strong suit nor something they do on a regular basis. They seem more inclined to see where the road takes them as opposed to charting a path.

There are several reasons for this. HR professionals admit that they are so busy helping their clients with their careers that there is not much time left for themselves. Also, they maintain that it is easier to play an "assist" or coaching role for someone else as opposed to developing a plan of their own. Again, this is the theme of helping and supporting others that is part of the HR psyche. However, the focus on careers falls short when it comes to us (HR professionals).

How Is Career Planning in HR Different?

Rarely does Human Resources have the same head count or funding that other departments might have in career planning. While our clients may have had funding to support training, career counseling, and mentors to develop their teams, it is unlikely that Human Resources will get an equal share. When succession planning, mentoring, or other company-wide programs were implemented, generally the focus was on getting the internal clients trained on these tools, with Human Resources being the afterthought by, ironically, Human Resources. Perhaps the assumption has been that Human Resources could take care of itself when it comes to services such as training and career development they are providing for the rest of the organization.

One of the last hurdles for Human Resources is our own lack of self-respect and discomfort with self-promotion. It is the quaint notion that bragging is the exclusive domain of the sales team. The superstars in sales, marketing, and logistics may not really contribute more to the success of their organization compared to what Human Resources has done, but they are just more vocal about it. People see what they do because they bring attention to their own accomplishments and they communicate them in a way that relates to success of the business. As Human Resources explains its strategic value and unique insights to the C-Suite, we need to internalize this argument with external means.

Then there is all the informal activity that supports career growth in the organization. Counterparts in other functional groups tend to be invited to a steady stream of corporate events, golf and other outings where informal alliances are made, mentor-protégée relationships are cemented, and lasting career connections are established. Yes, there are companies that hold meetings for their HR leaders where career topics may be covered or where HR speakers may be brought in to cover these topics. However, these are not in the same frequency, depth, and regularity as activities experienced by our clients in other functional areas. As noted earlier, the clients we serve are generally better funded to engage in these kinds of events while Human Resources is often subject to tight budget restraints and heavy work schedules. These restrictions may occur because Human Resources is not a revenue-producing group or profit center in most companies.

To maintain a balanced view, there are some examples of companies that have structured career management programs for their HR practitioners, although generally this is not the case. Cingular Wireless developed a "STAR" program with 360-degree assessments and business mentoring components for its HR generalists, which was expanded to include HR specialists. The program was well received and helped retain HR professionals during times of merger integration.

Bob Knight, development manager of Cisco Systems in Atlanta, says his company requires employees to have formalized development plans, which are reviewed annually by their manager and business partner. Knight admits that this process is not followed in Human Resources. He also admits that HR professionals are last in line for developmental planning and that more work in this area is needed. Cisco does provide plenty of technical training, and sponsors HR professionals for membership in SHRM, The American Society for Training

& Development (ASTD), and other professional organizations. On a selective basis, their high-potential HR professionals receive opportunities to attend MBA programs at Stanford, Wharton, and the University of Michigan, which are specifically targeted to their educational needs. Cisco did offer a "Career Connections" workshop, which was adapted for Human Resources to evaluate leadership competencies.

Human Resources is generally so caught up with the need to service its clients in the face of constantly shrinking resources, that career planning for HR professionals "falls by the wayside." With Human Resources struggling in these difficult financial times to stay afloat, avoid cuts in headcount, and prove its worth in the corporation, structured career planning programs, without a compelling and documentable cost-benefit upside, would no doubt be considered a luxury.

In addition to a lack of focus and resources, there are other dynamics that explain why career planning presents unique challenges for the HR practitioner. As indicated previously, the HR office is a lonely place. As Human Resources is the keeper of confidentiality for the organization, the typical HR practitioner has limited outlets for discussion of sensitive topics related to their development. Certainly, one channel of support for HR professionals is their supervisors.

A survey published in 2007 shows that the HR staff get most of their career advice from their boss.[3] While this approach may be useful and timely, what happens when there are issues the practitioner does not want to discuss with the supervisor, or when the supervisor is part of the career challenges, or the feedback is dated and wrong? What happens when the boss does not support the career advancement of the professional? Practitioners would then have to find other sources in the company within Human Resources or they would have to take steps to find a trusted contact within the company or outside Human Resources in the community.

After seven years of working under a manager who encouraged career development and growth, the boss was promoted and one of the authors found herself working for someone who did not support her development. Recognizing that she needed to find another path, she reached out to her former boss and started working to develop relationships with HR professionals through her SHRM chapter. She got more involved in leadership roles — as a volunteer rising to president of the chapter and eventually positions on the state council, regional positions, and even a national committee role. All of these opportunities allowed her to develop her management skills. The social and professional networks she cultivated helped her continue to seek advice and support for managing her career and allowed her to seek opportunities eventually to move up and out of her organization.

The thought of looking inside your own organization for help may make you feel uncomfortable. The practitioner might not be inclined to pursue this route due to lack of time or concern about the risk. HR practitioners see themselves as the source of support to their clients on career and many other critical-business issues. They may be reluctant to ask these same sources for help, because such a request could be interpreted as self-serving and they may also fear their image might be tarnished in the eyes of their clients. In short, it is understandable why some HR practitioners end up "talking to themselves" or taking limited action on the topic of their own careers. With little in the way of guidance and resources, it is understandable how and why career planning for HR practitioners has historically taken a back seat.

The State of Your Career

HR practitioners should engage in career assessment at least semi-annually. The process is discussed in detail in Chapter 8.

Who Is Involved?

You need to be in charge of your career and the decisions affecting it. However, at its best, career planning is a collaborative process. While "to yourself be true" is valid, there are others who have touched your career who can be valuable resources in the process, and you should be gathering their input. Current and former bosses, peers, suppliers/vendors, business contacts, and friends and family members have different perspectives about you and know you in different ways. Career counselors and contacts at professional trade associations can help, too. In various parts of this book, we discuss networking contacts, mentors, coaches, and others who can contribute to shaping your career in a positive way. We suggest that you leverage them.

The Work/Life Juggle

One of the first things you need to do is establish your work/life priorities and be realistic about how you want to balance them. If you don't do this, you may find yourself burned out and ultimately unsuccessful. You may find that at various points in your life your career plans take detours.

If you are new to the workplace, perhaps you have a "sky is the limit" ambition. Maybe, a vice presidency or CEO role is on the horizon. You may have the time, energy, and ambition to take your career to the top. If you are in your 40s, married with children, and have aging parents who need attention, a less demanding career direction may work better for you. Finally, you may have modest career ambitions, may desire more personal time, or may be looking at developing a career transition into retirement and want to reserve a considerable amount of personal time. You'll need to look at the jobs that will support that priority, and understand the likely financial and career growth implications.

In addition to the job itself, think about required travel that might be part of a regional job, for example, and the impact that would place on your personal life. If you have a partner, spouse, or significant other with travel requirements for their own jobs, how will your career plans mesh? Fortunately, companies have become more flexible with telecommuting, flextimes, job sharing, etc., and technology is available to support it. Some HR roles do their work through a call center arrangement. However, we are in *Human* Resources, which means a certain amount of face time is a likely job requirement.

The key is to be honest with yourself. If you are motivated by money and want to go for higher paying jobs, there are sacrifices to make in terms of personal and family time. If you want to return to school for a graduate degree, you may seek out a slower path for a few years so you can juggle your job and career. Some industries require a faster pace. Compensation differences in these industries or alternative jobs need to be considered. Utilities or government agencies will move at a slower pace but not pay as well as a job in manufacturing, high-tech, or advertising.

Also, consider the seasonality of jobs. If you are considering a compensation or benefits role, for example, the planning cycle for the next calendar year occupies the fourth quarter and will generally put significant demands on your time. If that's the time of the year your children participate in cross-country soccer championships, you need to identify your priorities. Other jobs may have their particular seasonality to consider. If you work in manufacturing or in call center operations, think about the impact that shift work may have on your personal time.

Table 4.1 **Self-Assessment**

My Entry into HR	Date:
Education:	
Experience:	
Current Life Priority: Work ____ Play____ Health____ Family____ Community____ (Rate: 1-5)	
Values: (Rate H, M, L) High, Medium, Low	

New Experience _____	Cultural Opportunities_____
Leadership _____	
	Religious Conviction _____
Free Time _____	
	Recognition _____
Wealth _____	
	Geography _____
Responsibility _____	
	Power _____
Job Security _____	
	Change _____
Challenge _____	
	Friendship _____
Intellectual Growth _____	

Targeted Position:
Targeted Industry:
Target Culture:
People to Target:

What Does the Self-Evaluation Process Look Like?

Here are some questions you need to ask yourself. Use Table 4.1 to record your thoughts.

- How did I get here? What brought me to my current HR position?
- What resources do I have in the way of education and experience?
- What motivations are in play for me right now?

- What are my current life priorities: work, play, health, family, community?
- How much time and energy do I have to give?
- What things do I value the most? (*friendship, leadership, free time, wealth, responsibility, job security, family, challenge, fun, independence, creativity, new experience, cultural opportunity, religious conviction, adventure, recognition, geographical location, power, variety, change, intellectual growth*)
- What is happening in my personal/family life that could drive a career move (or not)?
- What kind of time commitment am I prepared to make for my career? Is the commitment constant, seasonal, or subject to other variables?
- Where do I want to go? (C-Suite, senior HR position, specialist, generalist, business role outside of HR, consulting, outsourcing, academia)
- What kinds of companies and industries am I interested in? What kind of company culture am I most comfortable in? (Some trial and error could be involved here.) Who can I consult to get this kind of information?

Here's what you need to know and the resources you need to have. Use Table 4.2 to get organized.

- Insights about your career strengths and satisfiers. (Where to go for this: past performance reviews, assessments, informal performance feedback received, reviewing past jobs and where you excelled or didn't, defining moments in your career.)
- Understanding of available careers — what's hot for today and tomorrow. Understand the differences between HR generalist and specialist roles in relation to responsibility and pay. (Where to go for this: SHRM web site, talent acquisition specialists, others in the position to make hiring decisions.)
- Knowledge of competencies required for your career interests. (Where to go for this: SHRM competencies.)
- Identify your support system. (Where to go for this: mentors, coaches, current or past bosses or peers you are comfortable with, business partners, educators, family/friends, people who are influential in your life, those who will be direct in a constructive and caring way. Assemble a "board of directors" that will carry you through your career.)
- The gaps between where you are and where you need to go. (Where to go for this: within yourself! Only you know the answers.)

Table 4.2 **Career Resources Checklist**

What	Where To Go
Career Strengths & Satisfiers	☐ Past Performance Review ☐ 360-degree Assessments ☐ Other Test Batteries ☐ Informal Feedback
HR Career Options	☐ SHRM Web Site ☐ Talent Acquisition Specialists ☐ Career Counselors ☐ Job Incumbents
Competencies for Targeted Job	☐ Job Postings ☐ Job Descriptions ☐ SHRM Competencies ☐ Job Incumbents
Support Systems	☐ Business Partners ☐ Network Contacts ☐ Friends, Family
Gaps	☐ Education ☐ Knowledge ☐ Skills

Determinations You Need to Make

- To what degree is your career situation satisfying your needs, wants, and values?
- Are you happy with the status quo or is a change needed?
- What steps am I able/willing to make at this time?
- Who can help?
- What do I want to accomplish in the next six months?

Generalist vs. Specialist Roles

There are pros and cons for being a generalist or a specialist. In addition, if you want to switch from one to the other, you need to think about how you might navigate between the two. For example, it might be reasonable for a compensation analyst to move into a benefits role, but more difficult to move into a generalist role. A generalist will have difficulty moving into a specialist role unless he or she can show a concentration in one or two functional areas. Today, it appears to be a niche market with many opportunities open for specialty roles as companies become more sophisticated. Pay ranges will also differ based on the role.

Actions to Take

- We recommend that HR practitioners do a career assessment or meet with a mentor semi-annually.
- Complete the HR Travel Itinerary (see Appendix).
- Establish a "witness or partner" to your plan.
- Get serious about working the plan and following up.

What are the Possible Challenges Related to Your Career Plan?

There are possible roadblocks you might encounter along with some possible solutions. Use Table 4.3 to plan your next moves.

1. *Career is not moving according to your time table within your company or externally.* **ACTION:** Analyze the cause. Is it knowledge or education, or an interpersonal skills issue? Consider 360-degree or other assessment.
2. *Limited resources for education and training, and difficulty in finding a coach or mentor.* **ACTION:** Check the web sites of professional associations for free educational sessions, webinars, blogs, and chat rooms. Look into a relationship with a mentor.
3. *Economic factors with your current employer or externally inhibit the movement you are looking for.* **ACTION:** Volunteer for special projects (internally or in the community), committees, and consider a possible lateral move or demotion to get the experience you want. Engage the help of your supervisor and/or peers to get some insight on this problem. Strategically consider the value of personally funding some needed training or development.
4. *Family, health, and personal issues are taking center stage.* **ACTION:** You may need to delay or postpone your plans until things settle down. Be careful not to use this as a crutch for taking needed action.
5. *Lack of time to make the career plan happen.* **ACTION:** Make appointments with yourself to focus on your career and take it seriously. Block off your calendar and attach the same importance as if you were meeting with

a client. Engage the help of friends, colleagues, networking contacts, mentors. (See Chapter 7 for developing a board of directors.)

6. *You find yourself unemployed.* **ACTION:** No excuse now. This is the perfect time for working on your career. (See Chapter 11 for more details.)

7. *Your goal is to change or modify your role within Human Resources, and you are overshadowed by those who are currently more qualified than you.* **ACTION:** Talk to the people who were successful to learn about tactics that worked for them. Volunteer to help them in their new role.

8. *Difficulty in developing the proper motivation to manage through the career plan.* **ACTION:** Analyze and talk with others you trust to get to the root cause of the problem. Look for trends. Has this happened before? Perhaps you are not comfortable or committed to the plan.

Table 4.3 **Troubleshooting Challenges**

Issue	Planned Action	Date
Career not Moving According to Plan		
Limited Opportunity for Education & Training		
Economic Opportunities Impede Movement		
Family/Health Issues		
Lack of Time for Career Plan		
Unemployed Status		
Competition from More Qualified Candidates		
Motivation Issues		

Final Thoughts

- Developing your own career plan can be a challenging process which can take weeks or months.
- It involves lots of soul searching and being honest with yourself and those close to you about what you really want.
- It can be painful too, as some of us force ourselves into the mold that others want for us instead of what *we* want for ourselves.
- Getting to the "moment of truth" can be a real awakening.
- The benefits of developing the discipline to regularly review your career itinerary are overwhelming.
- We've seen professionals who have spent years in an inappropriate career niche; they knew they were unhappy but didn't know why. The ripple effects for their family members were far reaching.
- Mastering these skills will not only help you personally but will prepare you to offer better coaching for those you serve.

Preparing to Embark

*Bob and Susie are attending a conference sponsored by an HR orga-
nization. Both have a few years of experience in Human Resources,
as well as education that included HR courses. Susie asks Bob, "Do
you like HR?"*

*"I like it but I'm starting to get a little bored with recruiting. We
have a high turnover rate, which makes me think I have job security," Bob jokes. He goes on to say, "I wonder why we have the turnover we do and I'd like to be part of fixing the problems that may be
causing it."*

*"I know what you mean," replies Susie. "I'm sure there is more to
being an HR professional, but I'm not sure what competencies I need
to have or what standards I need to be successful in the future."*

*"Yes," Bob agrees, "I think I need to know more to even decide if
I want to stay in HR."*

What Is a Competency?

"While universal agreement has yet to be reached, there appears to be growing
consensus that a competency is a collection of related knowledge, skills, abilities, and other personal characteristics (KSAOs) working in concert to produce
outstanding performance in a given area of responsibility. A competency affects
a major part of one's job (one or more key roles or responsibilities), correlates
with performance on the job, can be measured against well-accepted standards,
and can normally be improved through training and development. Once ad-

equately defined, competencies provide a firm foundation on which an organization can build a fully integrated performance management system."[1]

Though a number of authors and experts have identified their list of competencies, in our experience, there are a set of core standards that are essential for a successful career in Human Resources.

Recognizing Competency-Based Behaviors

Assess yourself as you read this chapter. Do you have these competencies? Observe the behavior of others in your organization to see if they demonstrate the competencies. Look at the most successful individuals in your organization and others in both Human Resources and other management roles. What competencies do they have? Consider talking to them about how they developed their competencies, what jobs they've held, and their education and experience.

As we discuss each competency, we've identified some behaviors that might indicate whether an individual has that competency.

Use Table 5.2 at the end of the chapter to assess your HR competencies.

Strategic Visionary

As the HR profession has evolved to be an important element of organizations, it has become clearer that HR professionals need to have strategic vision. *Being able to see beyond the functional day-to-day* is a critical competency for most successful professionals.

For example, let's say that Bob could see his company's staffing methods are not consistent with the job market conditions. With this perspective, he could gather data to determine the reason the company is experiencing significant turnover. He could then change his approach and help the company be more successful. On the other hand, if the rate of turnover is somehow tied to the company's strategy, and if there is value in continuous new talent for some reason, he could better support it and not be frustrated.

In an age of extreme global competition, *and* where one company can easily copy the processes, products, raw materials, and market strategy of another, the only true difference in the success factor is the human capital. Having the right people in the right jobs at the right time, as Jim Collins says, makes the HR function valuable.[2]

However, to create value for business, the HR professional needs to understand how to look at everything through a strategic lens.

HR professionals need to be able to make strategic business decisions and develop HR strategic plans that align with the plans of the organization. In order to do this, all levels of Human Resources must know what the business does to make money. They must know who the customers are, what their buying habits are, who the competition is, and where the company is going in the future. This is criteria for everyone in the organization; the lack thereof is generally the reason for failure if the key people don't have a real handle on these questions. Unfortunately, Human Resources has been accused of not having this focus.

Behaviors Indicating Strategic Vision

- Always looking at how actions impact the total organization or the future
- Asking how a decision relates to the values of the organization
- Demonstrating an interest in how things work in all areas
- Finding connections between parts of the organization
- Seeking out the expertise of others and recognizing gaps in information

---

Coach

Coaching is the ability to help another do what is needed to be successful. Sometimes it means giving direction, but most often it means being able to see the talents, abilities, and shortcomings of another and helping them see those things so that they can do what it takes to be successful. Coaching also helps in influencing behaviors necessary for employees to meet goals or targets.

You don't necessarily have to have the same skill level as the person you are coaching to be a good coach. In fact, if you think about many coaches in sports, they were often not the best players themselves. What they could do was bring out the best in others.

A good coach gives guidance and reflects back to the individual what they are doing well and what needs to be improved.

To be a good coach you need to be able to establish trust and credibility with those you are coaching. You need to be able to delegate responsibility and be comfortable in doing so. You need to accept the fact that you are not directly responsible for the results.

Being a coach may involve helping a supervisor deal with a problem employee vs. stepping in and resolving the problem, even when solving it would be easier. The positive result is a stronger supervisor who can solve the next problem on their own. In addition, the relationship between the supervisor and the employee can be enhanced, and the resulting trust means a more effective operation.

Behaviors Indicating Coaching Strength

- Develops others
- Offers challenging assignments with guidance but allowing the other to do the work
- Asks questions like, "How would you approach that?" or "How could we solve that?"
- Is trusted by others
- Likes to see others get recognition and succeed
- Is a good listener

Advisor

To be an advisor, you need to have expertise in a subject-matter area. HR professionals should have depth in their HR technical knowledge so that they can provide advice to the organization. Just as the marketing department or the IT department professionals should be the experts in their fields, Human Resources should know its stuff.

This means that even if you intend to work at a higher management level, though you need to develop your strategic management skills, you still need to have some functional HR knowledge.

You don't have to be an expert in compensation, for example, but you need to have the basic understanding of the functional area, as well as a sense for when you need to ask questions or look for resources. For example, Bob the HR manager may know that the computer programmers in his company are being paid as exempt employees. He should know about the Fair Labor Standards Act and the applicable wage and hour laws so that he can check if the computer programmer positions are properly classified. Bob needs to know where to go and look for the answers, or to which of his employees he could delegate the research.

If you don't have the information, knowledge, or skills needed to advise the individual or the organization on HR topics, you will not be a successful HR professional.

It is important to remember that an advisor provides the information, but is not in a position to control the outcome. As an advisor, you need to be able to provide the best advice to organization management — and then let go. This poses a challenge, because the HR commitment to ethics may not be shared by all management.

When it comes to being an advisor, you have choices and obligations, including reporting activities that you believe are dangerous — or illegal — to the authorities, giving advice and moving on, responding to the actions of the management, or even leaving the organization if you disagree with the direction the organization takes.

Ultimately, to be a good advisor, you need to be respected (and therefore sought out for your knowledge). You also need to be able to clearly present information or advice to the audience you are advising. If you are to have an impact, you also need to be able to translate the information into business language or marketing language, or operations language or union language.

Behaviors Indicating Advisor Strength

- Known by all as the go-to person for HR issues
- Lifelong learner – always seeks ways to learn more
- Great communicator; can talk to anyone
- Is motivated by the success of the project vs. own success
- Nonjudgmental

Influencer

Influencing is different than coaching and advising. It involves getting people to do things differently — changing behaviors. These behavioral changes require that the individuals, employees, managers, clients, etc., have both the ability to perform new behaviors and the motivation. Influencing requires you to look at the personal, social, and structural aspects of the situation. Once you have analyzed the situation from those angles, you can then provide the training, rewards, and environmental changes that will get people to perform the desired behaviors.[3]

To be an influencer, you need to: have good analytical and problem-solving skills; be able to work with others to develop ideas; and understand how the human mind works. Empathy and strong interpersonal skills, as well as the ability to energize individuals and groups, are important. Finally, good planning skills (to put all of the pieces together), including determining costs and return on investment, are necessary if you are going to change behaviors in the organization.

Human Resources should be the recognized leader in influencing changes in the organization, since it shares this responsibility for the people aspects of the business.

Behaviors Indicating Influencer Strength

- Understands the feelings and motivations of others
- Good planning skills
- Change-management skills
- Superior interpersonal communication and persuasive skills

Administrator

Since the roots of Human Resources are in the administrative aspects of business, we often go to extremes to shed that image. There is a danger, however, in rejecting all administrative work. A large number of small- and mid-sized businesses have HR positions that can't avoid the administrative aspects of the job.

In addition, while human risk may be a key player in risk management, document management, recordkeeping, and various legal and regulatory filings, etc., the fact of the matter is that most white-collar jobs have a significant element of administrative responsibilities.

The key to managing administrative functions effectively is to take advantage of the tools that make this more basic work manageable, such as knowing how to use standard computer applications, and HRIS systems to effectively track and manage data. You need to maintain a basic working knowledge and understanding of these systems. Also, it is critical to maintain networks and sources for help from internal and external experts.

Outsourcing the administrative aspects is fine too, but you still need to know how to:

- Define your needs.
- Establish a budget.
- Use a Request for Proposal (RFP) process to choose the right provider.
- Manage the supplier, including establishing ongoing benchmarks and planned review, and new RFP solicitations.
- Ensure regular follow ups and audits are done, and take action when initiatives are late or not according to plan.

Behaviors Indicating Administrator Strength

• Good at manipulating data	• Likes detail
• Well organized	• Setting priorities
• Brings order to chaos	• Multi-tasking
• Analytical person	

Problem-Solver

Since Human Resources is the balance point between the organization and the employees, to be successful in a HR career, you need to be adept at solving problems. For example, helping an employee (with a sick family member) who is missing work to understand the impact on the organization is as important as helping the organization retain a good employee without great losses.

Problem-solving has many aspects. Like many skills, the more we practice problem-solving, the better we get at it. You need to be comfortable with multiple approaches to solving a problem.

Consider developing your skills:

- Decide which problems are worth solving.
- Take one step at a time — start with the first, most obvious, part to solve and, after some successes, move onto the more complex issues.
- Break it down — divide a large problem into smaller, more manageable problems.
- Use the scientific method — form a hypothesis and develop experiments to test the hypothesis.
- Implement trial and error — just keep trying different approaches till you find one that works.
- Brainstorm — list all ideas, even those that seem ridiculous, then evaluate the solutions and toss out or combine ideas to come up with a solution.
- Look for the root cause — look behind the face of the problem to determine the true cause.

Behaviors Indicating Problem-Solving Strength

- Determining which problems are most pressing
- Looks for challenges and difficult situations
- Tenacious
- Has good objective judgment and doesn't base decisions on feelings alone

---

Advocate

To be a good HR professional, you need to be an advocate for both the employees and the company.

Advocacy requires the ability to speak out or act in the best interest of one group or another. It is also:

- Questioning situations, status quo
- Recommending solutions

- Providing support (with diplomacy)
- Participating in organizational planning and process development
- Representing a side or group that is not being treated according to policy, law or ethics
- Applying your HR expertise to problem resolution
- Putting your group (client) ahead of yourself

Advocacy can be for an individual, a group, or an organization. Advocacy involves being brave enough to put yourself on the line.

Behaviors Indicating Advocacy Strength

- Steps up – speaks up for what is best for the organization and the people
- Looks for evidence and data to support decisions
- Has good presentation skills
- Persuasive
- Has strong interpersonal skills

Metrics Keeper

Since, in business, often "what gets measured, gets done," HR professionals are often the facilitators, or keepers, of the measures. Like the CFO, we may be the function that polices the measuring of success factors — particularly when it comes to the human side of the business.

This requires an understanding of what to measure, how to measure, when to measure, and why to measure factors in the organization. Knowledge and application of basic statistics and probability is important, as is the ability to apply analytics to the results and to the success of the business.

It is critical for Human Resources to understand how a balanced scorecard helps everyone in an organization focus on predetermined success factors.

One HR professional we know revealed that 40 percent of her performance was based on customer satisfaction, even though she rarely saw a customer! Understanding how customer satisfaction relates to Human Resources, and keeping track of it, helped her focus on the core values and mission of the company.

Sometimes you are responsible for metrics over which you have little or no control.

Behaviors Indicating Metrics Strength

- Likes analysis, working with data
- Can translate outcomes into numbers
- Understands how metrics impact the goals of the organization
- Ability to create, manage, and interpret relational databases

Protector

Human Resources often takes the lead in protecting the organization's reputation. Though all managers must participate in this initiative, Human Resources plays an important role, since we are responsible for the people and their behavior. Unethical or illegal behavior hurts the organization's reputation and the people both inside and outside the organization.

On the other hand, we need to be careful not to hide behind the role of protector. As HR professionals, we must remain aware of the balance between the focus and the behaviors, and how they line up with the laws and ethical values. At the same time, we must always keep the business goals and needs in mind.

Being good role models in our own behaviors, maintaining up-to-date understanding of legal issues, and applying out advocacy roles are ways we demonstrate our protector aspect.

Behaviors Indicating Protector Strength

- Demonstrates commitment to the organization
- Personal ethical behaviors
- Interested in and informed about the legal issues
- Research-oriented

Alliance Builder

Human Resources is given the responsibility to balance the needs of the organization with those of the people in the organization. This provides the HR professional with a great opportunity to be an alliance builder.

Building alliances requires the ability to discern the perspective of others, while not necessarily agreeing with everything. Demonstrating respect for all individuals is the key to building alliances for the HR function (and to assisting others to build alliances).

If HR professionals want to build partnerships and alliances, empathy — and the ability to value talent while assessing behaviors — is key. They must be able to respect the person and see their strengths but also hold them responsible for performance and behaviors that contribute to the success of the organization.

Having strong communication skills, good objective judgment, and the ability to put it all together allows the HR professional to facilitate and initiate change that will help the organization to build alliances.

Behaviors Indicating Alliance-Builder Strength

- Likes to solve resolve conflict
- Can see both sides or multiple sides to the issue
- Demonstrates an empathy with others
- Balances decisions with good objective judgments and bases things on information
- Likes working with people issues
- Successfully brokers strong partnerships among people
- Ability to determine the priorities of others
- Persuasive

Different Roles Need Different Competencies

The preceding information is by no means exhaustive. There are probably other competencies of value available for you to be successful in your HR career.

It is important to recognize that although the aspects listed apply to all HR roles, some are more critical for certain career goals. For example, if you don't have highly developed strategic vision, you could not be a successful CHRO. Table 5.1 suggests some matchups for various positions.

How Do You Develop a Competency?

Since a competency is "a collection of KSAOs," there are a number of things you can do to develop yourself professionally.

Knowledge can be acquired by study, formal and informal education, reading, and discussing with experts and knowledgeable people. Skills are developed by applying knowledge and learning to activities. Practice and experience can help you develop a competency.

The other two factors that make up competencies are more impacted by your personality and natural talents or thinking styles. If you are a number person vs. a word person, you may be able to achieve a higher level of proficiency as an administrator. Personal characteristics are also an important part of each competency. In other words , due to your personality, you may not be able

Table 5.1

Competency	Critical for:	Valuable for:	Basic for all HR
Strategic Vision	CHRO	HR Manager	
Coaching	HRD/OD/ Manager	Employee Relations	
Advisor	Manager	Compensation/ Benefits	
Influencer	CHRO & all Managers		X
Administrator		Mid-level Specialists	X
Problem- Solver	CHRO		X
Advocate	Managers		X
Measures Facilitator	CHRO & Managers	All HR Jobs	
Protector	CHRO & Managers	All HR Jobs	
Alliance Builder	CHRO & Managers	All HR Jobs	

to reach the highest possible level. For example, being strong in administration requires an individual who is detail-oriented. If you are not a detail-oriented person by nature, you may never be able to be as strong as someone else in that area.

While you may not be able to change your nature, you may be able to learn new behaviors so that you can be at a good level in a necessary competency. One HR professional we interviewed had problems with numeric reasoning. He realized that, to be effective in HR management, he had to learn more about dealing with numbers and he had to learn techniques for dealing with detailed data. He also developed strategies for surrounding himself with people who had strong competencies that he lacked, and he learned how to converse intelligently about administrative aspects.

Understanding that you may never reach the highest levels in some areas may help you decide how reasonable a particular career path might be for you. If you don't have a natural bent toward strategic vision, for example, you may want to direct your career planning away from the highest levels of HR management.

Final Thoughts

- You need some general competencies to be successful in any HR job.
- Certain specialties or positions require specific competencies.
- Strength in all areas is not necessary for every job.
- If the information in this chapter makes you wonder if you need to look for a different career path, you might need to do just that.

Table 5.2

Competency	Behavioral Indicators	Self-Assessment
Strategic Visionary	Always looking at how actions impact the total organization or the future	
	Asks how a decision relates to the values of the organization	
	Demonstrates an interest in how things work	
	Finds connections between parts of the organization	
	Seeks out the expertise of others and recognizes gaps in information	
Coach	Develops others	
	Offers challenging assign-ments with guidance but al-lows the other to do the work	
	Asks questions like, "How would you approach that?" or "How could we solve that?'"	
	Is trusted by others	
	Likes to see others get recog-nition and succeed	
	Is a good listener	

continued on next page

Table 5.2 (continued)

Advisor	Known by all as the go-to person for HR issues	
	Lifelong learner: always seeks ways to learn more	
	Great communicator; can talk to anyone	
	Is motivated by the success of the project vs. own success	
Influencer	Understands the feelings and motivations of others	
	Good planning skills	
	Change-management skills	
	Very good interpersonal communication	
Administrator	Good at manipulating data	
	Well organized	
	Brings order to chaos	
	Analytical person	
	Likes detail	
Problem-Solver	Looks for challenges and difficult situations	
	Tenacious – doesn't give up easily	
	Has good objective judgment and doesn't base decisions on feelings alone	
Advocate	Steps up/speaks up for what is best for the organization and the people	
	Looks for evidence and data to support decisions	
	Has good presentation skills	
	Has strong interpersonal skills	

continued on next page

Table 5.2 (continued)

Metrics Keeper	Likes working with data	
	Can translate outcomes into numbers	
	Understands impacts of activities on the goals of the organization	
Protector	Demonstrates commitment to the organization	
	Has high ethical standards	
	Interested in and informed about the law	
	Research-oriented	
Alliance Builder	Likes to solve disagreements	
	Can see both sides	
	Demonstrates an empathy with others	
	Balances decisions with good objective judgments and bases things on information	
	Likes working with people issues	

Skills for
Career Travelers

Wanda is an HR business partner in a large energy company. She has not worked in several years, as she chose to stay at home to take care of her young family. As the day of her scheduled return to work gets closer, she is wondering about which skills she will have to hone.

There are certain skills that HR professionals should have in order to both manage their careers and perform their jobs. In Chapter 2, we summarized perceptions from senior-level leaders about where Human Resources needs to focus. Based on those insights, and what we have observed in our respective careers, we have summarized what we believe to be the most important skills.

In this chapter, we will discuss some critical skills that HR professionals need to develop. Table 6.1 will help you assess your proficiency for each of these skills. Read this chapter before filling out the table, so that you have an idea of the skills that will be discussed.

The table will help you identify which areas require work on your part and how you can plan to improve in each area. Give particular consideration to the skills which are most critical in your current or desired future career goals. It is also a good idea to go back to prior performance appraisal documents, 360-degree assessments, or any other feedback mechanisms to see if any of these have come up either as strengths or an area needing improvement.

Some of these skills may be addressed as a part of your formal education and training. Equally valid is learning you receive on the job or from observation. Think about people you encounter at meetings, conferences, and in one-on-one interactions who excel at these skills. These contacts can be role models. Alternatively, focus on those who fall short in these areas. It is also helpful to concentrate on people currently in the public arena or throughout history to assess how they mastered these skills. Sometimes you can improve your ability in some of these categories simply by watching and observing those who do it well.

For example, in the area of *negotiations* skills, do you know anyone who recently settled a labor contract? Learn more about the terms of the negotiations, what the trade-offs were, and how the opposing sides came to terms. For self *marketing*, focus on people you know who have high visibility, have been recently promoted, or have been assigned to coveted roles. Once you give it some thought, you'll probably find that it didn't happen by accident. They mastered one or more of these skills.

Table 6.1 **Skills Self-Assessment**

Skill	Value (High-Medium-Low)	Self-rating	Role Model	Action Plan
Self-Marketing	Importance today: H M L Importance in future: H M L	Novice _____ Skilled _____ Master _____		
Networking	Importance today: H M L Importance in future: H M L	Novice _____ Skilled _____ Master _____		
Interviewing	Importance today: H M L Importance in future: H M L	Novice _____ Skilled _____ Master _____		
Negotiating	Importance today: H M L Importance in future: H M L	Novice _____ Skilled _____ Master _____		

continued on next page

Self-Marketing

Many people in Human Resources have relationships with internal clients who are involved in marketing and sales initiatives. However, while they may observe how products and services are marketed and sold, few HR professionals have been exposed or trained to the concept of marketing themselves, and fewer still have actually executed and have been held accountable for marketing plans. Also, we have found that HR professionals are reluctant to sell themselves professionally. They prefer not to brag or boast. They see their role as enablers or supporters of others and are not comfortable with the concept of self-promotion. They may even think that they would be disappointing those they service since this is not typical HR behavior.

If you are not engaged in *self*-marketing, you'll need to accept that it won't happen. This is an activity that no one can do for you. Self-marketing is a critical behavior in developing your career. Everyone has the right and responsibility to promote themselves. As long as the self-marketing campaign is ethical,

Table 6.1 **Skills Self-Assessment (continued)**

Skill	Value (High-Medium-Low)	Self-rating	Role Model	Action Plan
Business Mind-set	Importance today: H M L Importance in future: H M L	Novice _____ Skilled _____ Master _____		
Influencing	Importance today: H M L Importance in future: H M L	Novice _____ Skilled _____ Master _____		
Presentation	Importance today: H M L Importance in future: H M L	Novice _____ Skilled _____ Master _____		
Tech Knowledge	Importance today: H M L Importance in future: H M L	Novice _____ Skilled _____ Master _____		

and individuals have integrity and are genuine in promoting their accomplishments, there will be dividends for the professionals who practice self-marketing techniques. After all, marketing is the way to explain why one product/service/person is *better* than another — it is a means to establish a competitive advantage.

Who will know what you have done unless you tell them? You are your own agent or campaign manager. Self-marketing is part of being responsible for your own career. It is not enough for only your friends or family members to know about your achievements. In today's competitive world of high technology, you never know the career impact of the next person you talk to. Unfortunately, unless you are engaged in self-promotion, you will be out run in your passive attempts to propel your career.

Realities of Self-Marketing for HR Professionals

- You need to be constantly aware of the image you are projecting, both on the job and in the community. Jeering at the opponent at a local ball game or having one too many beers in a public setting are not acceptable.
- Whether you like it or not, you have high visibility as the member of the HR team and a representative of the company.
- Human Resources is subject to higher standards than counterparts in other functional groups, as they are frequently perceived as the keepers of the company values and policies.

Behaviors You Can Practice to Promote Your Career

- Once you understand the facts, take positions on important company issues and interests.
- Have a cause or "campaign issue" that helps the organization meet its strategic goals. It should be a cause that you want people to associate you with, such as sustainability or keeping the company "green." Keep your "cause" neutral and nonpolitical, nonreligious, etc., unless you are working for an organization that is part of that cause, such as a church or political organization.
- Be appropriately assertive and forceful in verbal and written communications. Back up what you say with facts. Develop a sense of when to push back and when to compromise your position.
- Be objective and consistent (without being excessively rigid) in the positions you take. Do not allow your personal values, religion or politics to get in the way.
- Represent yourself and your company in the best possible light.

- Volunteer for task forces, committees, and other groups that are dealing with company issues. Deliver on your responsibilities and make sure your views are well known.
- Associate with strong leaders, and support those who legitimately need your help.
- Be active in the community and volunteer for worthy charities. You may want to make sure your community service is not contrary to your company's mission.
- Look for opportunities to write and speak about issues. Consider writing a white paper on a HR topic, commenting on a published article, or starting a blog. Be sure to check your company's policy on speaking out publicly or to the press. Most large companies have a structured process around pre-approvals for what you plan to communicate. Work with your public relations department on this (if you have one). Avoid potential embarrassment for you and your company.
- Seek out relationships (internally and externally) in areas of interest and visibility. Use other social networks to increase your visibility. (See Chapter 8.)
- Have a thorough understanding of where you want your career to go, and engage yourself in self-marketing actions to support that goal. If you are interested in getting into the nonprofit area, try doing some volunteer work there.
- Engage your mentor, coach, or boss (if appropriate) in your plan.
- Keep track of your accomplishments, including descriptions and metrics, and be sure they are reflected in resumes and bios.

Networking

Networking should be viewed as a tool to help implement your marketing plan and to help you achieve your career goals. While the term "networking" is overused and has different meanings to different people, it is basically about building and leveraging a contact base (see Table 6.2). The contacts can provide career advice to you over the course of your career.

Good contacts are based on mutual trust and support. For a variety of contacts, be sure to cast a wide net. These are contacts that can remain in your circle for your entire career, provided you continue to nurture them. Just like any other relationship, network contacts require care and feeding.

Technology has enabled us to identify and connect with a wide variety of people in our personal and professional lives. LinkedIn, Facebook, and other social networking groups have taught us how easy it is to stay in touch, as well as how publicly visible we are. Professional associations, including SHRM, may be introducing their own sites in the near future. Every business card you receive or person you meet is a potential networking contact.

One contact can lead to several others (or not). The idea is to keep expanding your network by being introduced to new people by the people you already know. You can use your network to get information, keep up-to-date on industry developments, debate HR best practices, build sources for the purpose of exchanging information, and more. In these instances, networking can be very satisfying and painless. If you know the right people, you will find out how quickly and easily you can get critical information.

Table 6.2 **Tips**

- Talk to people in business development and sales roles and other rainmakers. They are a great source of advice on networking and have large numbers of contacts.
- Consider sending end-of-year updates or holiday messages to your network.
- When you change positions (even if you remain with the same company), let your network know the most current information about your career moves.
- Be helpful and willing to assist others, such as when you are approached by a potential contact that needs your help.
- Don't wait for a crisis (i.e., job loss) to develop a network. Relationships are built on sharing experiences over time.
- Be respectful of the time of network contacts. Have a specific reason for your contact call and be able to clearly articulate how the person can help you. Be gracious and be sure to extend thanks to those who have helped you.
- Be sure to ask each contact how you can help them. Remember, a relationship is a two-way street.
- Keep good records about people who are in your network.
- Do not give out a name of a network contact without first getting their permission.
- Remember to protect confidential information that is shared with you.
- Networking is a two-way street. Participants expect you to provide ideas, resources, leads, etc., as often as they do.

Interviewing

When You Are the Interviewer

As an HR professional, it is most likely that you will use interviewing skills in the staffing arena, which is our focus in this chapter. However, keep in mind that there are other applications for interviewing: gleaning information about a new vendor or supplier you are considering, conducting an employee relations investigation where there are multiple witnesses, and getting to know a new work group you will begin to supervise, and so on.

We have found that some of the least effective job interviewers come from the HR ranks. Why is that? The role of the HR professional during the staffing process is often that of a gatekeeper, to rule out candidates who don't meet the basic job requirements.

However, the perception from those we have talked to is that they are merely checking qualifications off on a list and don't gain a true understanding of the knowledge and skills of the candidate. They don't look at transferable skills that could benefit the company. They need to spend more time exploring the cultural fit for management-level employees, as that is of equal or greater importance than the technical fit. We found that job seekers strategize on ways to circumvent or finesse the HR interview so that they don't become a casualty.

HR professionals can bring value to the organizations they serve by upgrading the quality of their interviewing skills, as well as those of the hiring managers they serve. By making more educated hiring decisions, the company benefits because:

- Hiring the candidate with the best job/cultural fit will lead to quicker assimilation to the company, improved morale, and higher productivity.
- Lower turnover and, as a result, lower recruiting costs.
- Enhanced company reputation and greater appeal to passive and active job seekers.

HR professionals who are effective interviewers practice behavioral interviewing skills to gain a better understanding of the candidate. With this perspective, they can make a more informed decision about whether or not to approve the candidate for the next step of the process. Behavioral interviewing skills can be easily learned. There are vendors that specialize in this type of interviewing, and they can teach these skills at your company or in public seminars.

Behavioral interviewing is based on the premise that past behavior predicts future performance. In advance of the interview, the interviewer will glean the key job components from the job description. They will then construct a series of questions to be asked of each candidate that will explore the candidate's knowledge or experience with that requirement. For example, if the job involves managing a staff, in addition to the basics of how many folks they have supervised and in what roles, the interviewer might ask the candidate to describe a situation where a performance issue developed with a direct report and how they handled it. The same question would then be posed to every candidate for the job. The answers would be scored by the interviewers, who need to be as objective as possible to avoid the risk of favoritism or discrimination. The candidate with the most number of points then should seriously be considered. Hiring managers would use the same process when candidates are passed on to them, with all the interviewers comparing notes at the end to decide who the best candidate is.

The *advantages* of behavioral interviewing are:
- Improved opportunity to get the best fit
- Logical, methodical approach to hiring
- Consistent process that holds up to legal challenges
- Improved camaraderie between Human Resources and the hiring managers on selection decisions

The *disadvantages* are:
- Time and money investment to learn the process
- Top-level support is needed; and must be done company-wide
- To be effective, Human Resources and their clients need to be committed and accountable to the process

Negotiating

Effective negotiation is a key skill for business and for life (see Table 6.3). We are all involved in many negotiations that occur during the course of the day, often without our realizing it. Some examples: negotiating a compensation package for a new hire, selecting a vendor for an HRIS package, and orchestrating a union contract. There is a dialogue, a give-and-take. Both parties present their needs, and a deal is struck. While we often relate negotiations to financial concerns, that is not necessarily the case. Negotiations can be about bartering for services, authority, accountability, or strategic mandates.

When the stakes are high, a formal structure for negotiations is often necessary. In the life of a HR professional who has responsibility for labor relations, being the chief spokesperson or on the bargaining committee calls for honed negotiations skills. In developing an agreement with a vendor or an outsourcer, a service-level agreement is often the format used to agree about costs, delivery time, and quality. In order to negotiate on an issue, each "side" needs to take a position. The negotiation is successful if all parties are able to come to terms.

HR professionals are sometimes criticized because they don't take positions on issues and/or don't aggressively defend their positions. To prepare for

Table 6.3 **Tips**

- Before entering a negotiation, decide what your bottom-line position is.
- Generate fresh ideas to help resolve conflicts or potential impasse.
- Maintain an open mind and keep the dialogue going. Use open-ended, nonjudgmental questions without being critical. Communicate that you are invested in reaching a mutually beneficial agreement for both parties.
- Read the nonverbal signs of the person you are negotiating with, and modify your position accordingly.
- Preserve the dignity of the other party. If you feel that resolution was in your favor, be professional and do not gloat. If you believe you did not prevail in meeting your goals, consider trying again at a later time, but refrain from being negative. Preserving the relationship may be more important than the results of the negotiation.
- "Wins" are not only financial. They can consist of time, flexibility, responsibility, and authority. Sometimes negotiations can involve bartering for services instead of money.
- Protect the interests of your organization – winning a deal may not be in the best interest of the company (depends on the terms), which may ultimately undermine your effectiveness and perceived value.

a negotiation, each side needs to understand what the other party is looking for and why. They also need to understand the value of both positions, be it quantitative or otherwise.

Asking for a raise or other monetary award, or resolving a compensation offer for a new job, can certainly be viewed as a negotiation. The individual asking for additional compensation needs to understand why the decision-maker might be opposed and must present a convincing argument as to why an increase is justified. A raise is less likely to be granted solely on the grounds that the requestor is hurting financially, has had a bad year, or is moving to a new home. Conversely, the chances that their request for a raise may be honored are greater if a cost-benefit analysis is presented. The requestor needs to show the value of their accomplishments and the impact to the bottom line where the company benefits (for example, if the requestor presents the case that they are responsible for lowering turnover and calculating a cost per head saved on replacements, hiring costs, or other expenditures).

In the case of a job offer, it is critical to research market data to see if it supports what you are asking for. If you are already being paid at or above market value, you would need to find another rationale for negotiating a higher salary. Also in this situation, you should know the value of the entire compensation package, if possible, as the whole is a sum of the parts. While the base salary may be below market value, the bonus or benefits package may be superior.

In summary, knowledge of the facts of your own position and those of the decision-maker are powerful tools in a successful negotiation.

Business Mind-Set

Your goal is to think like a business person and speak in terms that your internal customers will relate to (see Table 6.4). Your proposals and recommendations should be based on fact, demonstrating financial value, a return on the investment, and linkage to strategic goals. You should feel comfortable describing yourself as "a business person with a specialty in HR." The best way to acquire this mind-set is to shadow someone who is a recognized business expert. Ideally, this person should be in the same or related industry so you can carry the knowledge learned to your job. It might be a client, mentor, or a contact at another company. Let the person know what your goal is and where you are trying

---

Table 6.4 **Tips**

- Enlist the help of a mentor or coach who has the financial management expertise to work with you.
- Before you make a proposal or recommendation, put yourself in the position of your customer and client. Think about their view and what their objections will be. Be prepared to present your case in terms they can understand. Develop some alternate fall-back positions along with what differentiates them. Practice the presentation as often as it takes to be prepared and confident.
- Read business newspapers and periodicals like the *Wall Street Journal*, *Financial Times*, *Business Week*, *Fortune*, *Fast Company*, and the *Harvard Business Review*, and trade journals that pertain to your business. Pay attention to how business cases are presented.
- Follow the business section of your local newspaper, business chronicle, and chamber of commerce publications.
- Relate what you learn back to your job. Think about the impact to human assets and how your role might be affected. Perhaps an initiative may be needed as a result of something you learn.
- Read press releases, financial reports, and business results published by your company.
- Become an expert on what is happening in your industry. Pay attention to executive movement, mergers, acquisitions, and new product announcements. If possible, attend trade shows.
- Be inquisitive and ask intelligent, informed questions to expand your knowledge base.

to improve your knowledge. It might be in the areas of operations, finance, sales, or engineering.

You could ask this business expert to give you short assignments that would help you improve your knowledge of the business. They could help you learn how to develop and present a business case to support a position or recommendation. You could ask to go out on a sales call with this person or one of their direct reports. Another possibility is to be a participant in a meeting (i.e. financial review) that you normally don't attend as part of your HR role. The idea is to observe them in the process of doing their job.

The book *Financial Intelligence for HR Professionals* defines common financial terms and tools, and shows how to gauge your company's performance.[1] There is help on interpreting income statements and balance sheets. Information in the book will help you make better business decisions about staffing, budgeting, training, and other initiatives.

Persuasion

As an HR professional, much of your success comes from your ability to influence a broad range of people in the organization (see Table 6.5). If you have direct reports, you have innate "power" over them as part of your supervisory role. You also "control" their employment status, pay, job content, and, undoubtedly, many other things. However, when dealing with peers, clients, and contacts in other functional groups in the organization, you have no "control" over them and there is no reason that they have to respect or respond to you.

However, you need the support of these people in order to accomplish key components of your job. For example, how successful would you be at implementing a handgun policy in your organization without the backing of the management and supervisory levels? You would get the backing you need as a result of selling the benefits of having the policy and the risks of not having one. In essence, you would prevail by presenting meaningful arguments and being persuasive about why the policy is needed. As a result, the managers would actively support the policy and make it work.

As an HR professional, you have a responsibility to manage a balance between representing the needs of the organization and the needs of the employees. Maintaining this balance may mean that, at times, you don't have direct control over either side. The skill of influencing is critical in these circumstances.

People who have the ability to influence well build a base of followers and develop political "muscle." Others see them as a leader, someone they can trust and rely on. Good influencers are persuasive and are able to sell ideas.

Table 6.5 **Tips**

- Develop an active presence in your organization. Be visible on the manufacturing floor or in the sales office on a regular basis, instead of hiding in your office. Let people know you are accessible.
- Show others that you are genuinely interested in them as people and in their needs and concerns. Build your reputation as being open and flexible to a wide variety of people, opinions, and ideas. Encourage people to speak up, express divergent views, or controversial points. Offer them positive reinforcement for doing so.
- Demonstrate your honesty and integrity on a regular basis. Offer compassion and support when needed, but also defend the company view. By the positions and decisions you make, build a reputation for fairness. Let people know what you stand for and why.
- Choose your words carefully, anticipating in advance what the impact on the receiving end will be. Use tact and diplomacy when possible.
- Be known for coming up with creative solutions to thorny problems that are "win-win."
- In dealing with conflict, defend your point of view using factual information. Pick your battles around when to escalate or ask for an exception. Think about what your ultimate purpose is in doing so.
- Study leaders in your organization who have laudable persuasive skills. Ask them to share some of their techniques.
- In meetings, be sure to invite those who need to be there. Include those with a variety of views to ensure a meaningful discussion and best outcome. Be sure participants know your opinion and positions on issues and why.
- Develop an understanding of the motivations and abilities of individuals to determine if you can get them to do what you want them to do.
- Consider how you can change the structure or the environment to get people to change behaviors.

A good resource is the book, *The Art of Woo*.[2] The authors, G. Richard Shell and Mario Moussa, offer help around selling ideas through a four-step approach to assessing a situation, confronting the barriers, making a pitch, and securing commitments.

Presentation Skills

Being able to present to a group is a critical skill HR professionals should have (see Table 6.6). A presentation should educate or inform. The presentation should be geared to the audience.

Think about effective speakers you have seen and what made them effective. Conversely, you can also learn a lot from ineffective speakers.

Table 6.6 **Tips**

- Know your audience. Learn about their needs and wants, expectations, and hot spots in advance of the presentation.
- Before you start, engage the audience with an icebreaker, joke (keep it clean), or anecdote that relates to the topic. Another approach is to ask them what their expectations are for the presentation. You can record their expectations on a flip chart and then revisit it with the audience at the end of the presentation to ensure that their expectations are met.
- Be clear with your audience about the purpose of the presentation and the benefits they will gain from attending.
- Generally, a PowerPoint presentation works best with lots of white space, color and eye-catching fonts. There should be no more than a few bullet points on each slide. Use facts, figures, and examples to back up your points.
- Refrain from reading the slides; instead, talk about them in your own words, giving additional context to them.
- Estimate one minute per slide. Be sure you are under the allotted time that is provided or you will lose credibility with your audience. You are better off having fewer slides than will fit in the allotted time and allowing more time for questions and interaction from the audience.
- Practice, practice, practice.

Different people will have different presentation styles. In addition to content, how you present yourself physically, voice modulation, eye contact, and nonverbal gestures will affect the success of your presentation. There are thousands of books, videos, consultants, continuing education programs, seminars, and associations whose sole aim is to help people hone their presentation skills. Methods used include videotaping and providing a critique so you can practice and quickly improve your skills.

Technology, Data, and Where to Find It

The importance of technology cannot be understated in today's fast-moving world. Most companies no longer have the luxury of secretaries, typing pools, or other kinds of administrative support that existed in the past. Most employees are responsible for creating their own reports, charts, graphs, and for using e-mails to keep people connected 24/7.

There is also an increasing focus on metrics to track and measure HR value (see Table 6.7). Technology affords efficient and accurate data development, and eliminates the need for manual recordkeeping, which can be duplicative and prone to errors. In addition to technology and data, HR professionals need to know where to go to find information. They need to be familiar with periodicals, journals, reference books, and web sites (web chats, newsletters) for information. They should have knowledge of professional associations, trade groups, and consultants who can support them in their jobs. The Internet has made much information public knowledge. For example, many assessment tests that evaluate management styles are now prevalent on the web. As a result, there is significant opportunity for cost savings by using these online tools. In the past, access to these resources would have been a costly undertaking, but the ubiquity of online tools has mitigated this budget-busting problem.

Keep in mind that data and metrics are not an end but a means to getting important insights about the performance of Human Resources or your clients. Some HR professionals are guilty of accumulating data for data's sake. They should be synthesizing and analyzing this data to reach conclusions about how the operation is performing. For example, the use of data should be helpful in analyzing why voluntary turnover is so high, or why attendance or leave of absence trends are elevated.

Knowledge of word processing, spreadsheets, databases, presentation software, e-mail, and project management software is required for most HR jobs. Based on the position, additional knowledge may be needed for an Access database, and/or other in-house programs and systems. The field of HR information systems (HRIS) is a career unto itself.

HR professionals should be technology advocates who appreciate the capabilities of automation and technology to improve the productivity of routine workplace tasks. They should be looking to eliminate redundancy and paperwork, although sometimes doing so creates headcount reductions. This does not mean that they have to be technology experts, but they do need to understand capacity. For example, assuming there is a technology-driven HR information system in the organization, they need to be able to sell the benefits to their internal clients. If the organization has a relationship with an outsourcing vendor, the HR professional will have to be able to evaluate the performance of the vendor, understand contract terms, interview other clients of the vendor, and so on.

With the presence of generational gaps in the workplace, there may be some who are averse to switching to new technology, preferring to stick to the "tried and true" methods of the past. This resistance can occur within the HR group, as well as externally. The authors have experienced conversions to recordkeeping and timekeeping technologies. When we first converted to an HRIS system in one company, many internal clients were resistant because they believed they were taking on work that Human Resources should have been performing. Those who worked in technology (i.e., IT) were, on the other hand, eager to take on these duties as they understood the immediacy and flexibility in doing so. Based on their training, they were intellectually curious about learning a new system.

Table 6.7 **Tips**
• Use the technically savvy members of your organization to sell to "nonbelievers." Setting up a buddy system can be helpful during new systems conversion. Doing so will lighten the burden for you.
• Take advantage of technology options to eliminate routine or repetitive tasks. Learn to present the best business case for making the argument to convert to these systems.
• Take advantage of the wide range of training programs that are available online and in public seminars that can address any skill gaps you may have.
• Develop metrics that are vital to evaluating the performance of your group or department. Discuss these metrics with your clients to ensure they are onboard about the validity of using them. Consistently measure your output against these metrics; analyze and evaluate results.
• While knowledge of technology is important, do not hide behind it. There are some who will amass data for the sake of collecting it. Remember that the ultimate goal is to analyze and find the trends behind the data, applying it to improve business results.
• Be aware that bosses and clients may expect shorter turnaround times when it comes to reports and analysis because of the availability of information on the Internet.
• Develop a file system in your computer that will allow you to save and access information when you need it. Create folders to house information that you will need in the future. Encourage sharing of helpful web-based sources among direct reports, colleagues and clients.
• Before considering expenditure from a consultant, research available web resources to validate whether or not the expense is valid.

 Final Thoughts

- There are some key skills that you will need to leverage as a successful HR professional.
- Combined with your subject-matter knowledge of HR functional areas, these skills will put you in a good position to advance your career.

- Know how to market yourself.
- Develop networks inside and outside the organization.
- Develop your interviewing techniques.
- Become a top-notch negotiator.
- Grow your business mind-set.
- Work on becoming a persuasive business professional.
- Make sure that you have strong presentation skills.
- Be aware of the latest development in technology and data management, and learn how to find information using electronic tools.

Now, return to and complete Table 6.1. Update it on a regular basis. It will help to keep you grounded about where you are in each of these skill sets and, even more importantly, on where you need to go.

7

Partners on Your Journey: Mentors and Coaches

Susie is a compensation manager for a manufacturing company. She started as an HR coordinator and used the company tuition reimbursement program to complete her degree. Susie is at the point in her career where she would like to branch out to an HR-generalist role. She has spoken to her supervisor about making such a transition internally. However, the conversation did not really go anywhere. Susie knows she needs some guidance if she's going to continue to grow. She's not sure what to do. Susie is uncomfortable openly looking for help outside the company. After all, she's in Human Resources and expected to be a cheerleader for loyalty. Her supervisor is easy to talk to but is either unwilling or unable to provide her with guidance. The company talks about career development but doesn't have a formal program for anyone but the technical employees. Susie needs to find a trusted counsel.

We have discussed a number of tools and resources to help you determine your career path. However, your suitcase would not be complete without an understanding of what mentors and coaches can do to propel your career.

You can benefit from a mentor or coach at any career stage. You may need different kinds of mentors at different times, or you may find individuals who remain useful mentors throughout your career journey.

The Difference Between Mentoring and Coaching

The Brefi Group defines mentoring as "helping to shape an individual's beliefs and values in a positive way, often a long-term career relationship from someone who has 'done it before.' " They define coaching as "helping another person to improve awareness, to set and achieve goals in order to improve a particular behavioral performance."[1]

While a coaching relationship is usually arranged for a finite amount of time, a mentor relationship can extend over an entire career. Coaches will work with their subjects on improving performance or competencies in defined areas. For example, if a HR professional needs a tutorial on how sales compensation plans are structured to achieve business goals, they may engage a coach. In recent times, executive coaches have become more popular, and, in some cases, are considered to be a job "perk."

The coach can help the subject focus on a narrow area that may be impeding the individual's career advancement, possibly a performance or management-style issue. If the performance barrier can be overcome, the individual will be able to remain in their current position (if it had been at risk), or advance their career. Coaches are generally paid. Executive coaches can command a rate in the range of $100 to $500 per hour. The large spread in rates is based on the experience of the coach and whether or not they have established a particular specialty. In some cases, coaches are engaged by the company to work with a particular employee who is having performance issues, as well as with other employees as part of an advancement/succession program. In both examples, the company expects a payback on their investment.

The influence of mentors has a broader appeal. Mentors can offer a series of exercises, assignments, and informal counseling sessions that can be implemented over time to help develop their protégées. Some mentors delegate real business projects to their protégées and view the completion thereof as a form of payback for their mentoring services. Mentorships are developed more casually than coaching arrangements. Most mentors work for free. This situation is an advantage to the HR professional, as they can engage a mentor without enduring lengthy approval procedures, budget funding, etc. They can develop a relationship with a mentor independently and at any time.

The Use of Mentors and Coaches for Career Development

Some companies have formalized mentor programs that are organized and managed by Human Resources. These programs tend to be more successful than "one off" situations that are individually organized. The programs are run by people who have specialized knowledge of mentorships and have time to dedicate to this initiative. Also, since the company has committed resources to the program, a positive message is sent to employees. Some functional heads develop mentor programs with guidance from Human Resources.

Despite the prevalence of mentoring programs in many organizations, we find it rare for a HR professional to use these mentoring programs. One of the authors developed a mentoring program for HR managers in a Fortune 9 company. This was a "first time" event for Human Resources, although the use of mentors and coaches were not at all unique in other parts of the business. There were accolades from the HR professionals who used the program.

According to Chris Posti Tice of Posti & Associates in Pittsburgh, who provides executive coaching services, HR professionals don't view themselves as worthy of either coaching or mentoring services. The recurring theme of Human Resources being occupied with helping others at the expense of their own careers is at play here. They have a valuable and readily accessible resource available to them free of charge and they do not take advantage of it. Posti has been coaching for more than a decade, working with Human Resources as the broker between herself and the internal client groups. During that time period, she experienced only one occasion when an HR client asked about a coaching or mentoring tip for themselves. The benefits of coaching and mentoring from a business partner, according to Posti, are:[2]

Coaching

- Understanding the broader business implications of the companies they work for;
- Building more self-assuredness and having the courage to do the job the way the organization needs them to do it;
- Using creativity and out-of-the-box thinking;
- Prioritizing and coming up with defensible solutions; and
- Being open to advice (although it is not what they want to hear) — growing some "thick skin."

Mentoring

- Gaining a broader perspective by working with a different functional group;
- Increasing their visibility in the organization; and
- Learning to socialize outside Human Resources. Based on her experience, HR professionals are famous for "sticking with their own" during company social activities. During work hours, they tend to hibernate in their

offices and rarely get out for lunch or other events that would give opportunities for socialization. They pay a price for these behaviors when they try to build a network of contacts. (See Chapter 6 on Networking.)

The Benefit of a Mentor Relationship

The *Webster's New World Dictionary* defines "mentor" as a "wise advisor."[3]

As headcount and training budgets are reduced, business people are seeking alternate ways to improve performance, knowledge, or overall expertise. Considering the rapid pace of business in a competitive environment, supervisors have less time to spend with staff members to help them "get up-to-speed" on areas of self-development. For these reasons, the idea of engaging coaches and mentors has become more popular.

A mentor can be a guardian angel of sorts who can provide career and/or personal support for a specific period of time or "for life." It is someone with whom you can speak freely. A mentor will be in the position to give you valuable, constructive feedback delivered in a supportive way. If the mentor does not feel qualified to advise you on a particular matter, they may be able to recommend someone.

A mentor is a resource to help enhance an individual's performance, assist with their career progression, and fine-tune their knowledge and skill. A mentor is not intended for someone experiencing major performance issues. These issues are best addressed with the individual's supervisor, where a performance improvement plan is developed that might call for coaching, training, job shadowing, etc.

A mentor is different from a coach, who usually helps you attain a specific goal. A mentor is generally not your supervisor. Some supervisors have an affinity for mentoring, and the employees who report to them benefit greatly because of it. However, if you are starting from "scratch" looking for a mentor, you may not want to use your supervisor. A mentor will provide you objective feedback and advice in a specific subject area. A mentor does not have hiring, advancement, and firing authority over you as a supervisor does. Both you and the mentor enter the relationship voluntarily (no money is exchanged) and stay in the relationship for as long as it is working effectively or as long as both are committed to the relationship.

Latricia Smith, leadership development manager at AT&T, says,

> *Good mentors have three specific attributes: advise, advance, actuate. A mentor advises and recommends opportunities for continued development. As an advisor, a mentor provides gentle*

guidance to ideas and areas of development presented to them. Next the mentor is able to advance or champion the cause, using their network of influence and credibility to usher opportunities that will provide professional development for the protégé. The role of actuator for the mentor is the outward display of confidence and advocacy for the protégé. The mentor uses their influence in the organization, community and external networks to provide visibility and development opportunities for the protégé.

Figure 7.1

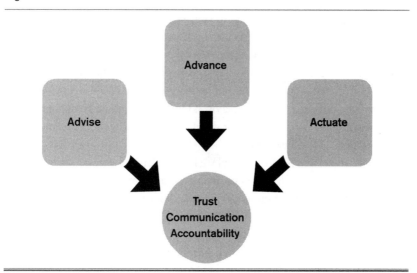

How Does Your Supervisor Fit into the Equation?

Your mentor can be a source of assistance on a broad base of matters, depending on their expertise. If, for example, you are experiencing challenges establishing or maintaining a good working relationship with your supervisor, your mentor may be able to provide you with some tactics for improving the situation. In other circumstances, your mentor may be able to work in tandem with you and your supervisor to attain a goal or specific accomplishment. Depending on the situation, you may feel more comfortable revealing sensitive information to a mentor than to a supervisor. However, you may be perfectly comfortable talking to your supervisor about your mentor.

While we can generally assume that supervisors have good intentions and are concerned about your career welfare, in reality there are some who may be threatened by your plans to advance your career. Latricia found that her efforts to advance in a growing manufacturing company were thwarted by her supervisor, who really was not interested in helping her career growth. With the guidance of a mentor, she decided she needed to leave the company and find another opportunity in a nonprofit organization — one that had significant opportunities in management. She was able to learn a lot about management on the job and then went on to assume more responsible management positions.

If you are part of an internal, company-sponsored, mentor program, there may be a requirement that your supervisor is apprised of your mentor relationship. If it is an external relationship, the decision of whether or not to reveal the mentorship to your supervisor is up to you. There are no requirements either way as long as your supervisor has not had a hand in selecting your mentor. Your supervisor may have some suggestions about how to go about finding a mentor. He or she may be able to suggest names of people who can be helpful to you. However, it is advisable for you to make the final decision on your own and without a direct tie to your supervisor. Ideally, they should be maintained as two separate relationships. A mentor should not be a barrier in the relationship with your manager and vice versa.

For example, an HR professional we know related this story. Maggie's supervisor was aware of her growing interest to learn more about HRIS as a career path and current trends in HR software applications. The interest was noted in her last performance review. The supervisor had a colleague at a former job that had substantial knowledge in this field and recently started a software firm. The colleague had a history of mentoring others who had interest in this field. The supervisor was able to connect Maggie to the colleague.

Some examples of issues a business mentor may be able to help you with include:
- How to chart the course of your career
- Deciding whether or not to change jobs or accept a specific opportunity
- Resolving sensitive situations or conflicts with people in the workplace
- Gaining knowledge or expertise about a specific subject matter
- Providing objective feedback on problematic situations
- Acting as a confidant and/or a sounding board for situations that arise in your career and being able to give you the proper perspective for them

If the mentor relationship lasts over a period of time, you will benefit, as the mentor will come to know you well. It can be a mutual growth relationship;

as you learn more and gain more experience, you can provide unique insights to the mentor. The mentor will be familiar with your strengths and areas of opportunity, and will know where you want to go from a career perspective. They will be able to vet patterns of behaviors on your part and provide a context for issues and decisions you have to make that affect your career. Since they are objective and have no "ax to grind," you will have the assurance that the advice you are given is genuine and in your best interest.

Identify the reason you want to have a mentor and the role you will want them to play. If you don't have a good sense about the kind of expertise you need, you might pick a mentor who is not qualified to meet your needs. The other risk is that the relationship may falter because it is lacking direction, and the mentor or the mentee can lose interest. Some folks are looking for a seasoned all-around business person who can help them navigate career issues. However, one of your goals might be that you want to attain a higher level of proficiency around finance — for example, you want to be able to read a balance sheet.

Finding the Right Mentor — Internal or External

In light of the important role the mentor will play in your career, the selection process should be approached deliberately. It could be time-consuming, as it can take some searching to find the right person. The most expedient path is to identify somebody within your company. The positives of this decision are that they are familiar with the environment you are operating in and may know some of the same people; they have a sense of internal political dynamics; and they likely have knowledge about your business cycles.

If your company has an internal mentoring program, look there first. There is probably one person or a group that is in charge of structuring and administering the program. Find out if you are eligible and how it works. Talk to people who have participated, and ask about their experiences. How long has it been in existence and what are the areas of focus? Learn how you get paired up with a mentor and if you can make your own selection. For example, you might say, "I've always admired Don and his leadership ability in the Engineering organization. I'd like the opportunity to approach him as a mentor for myself."

Despite the many advantages of participating in an internal program, there are no guarantees about program success. Joe Martucci, an HR executive based in Atlanta, tells about a mentoring program he managed involving high-potential employees: "Mentors volunteered, but pretty much at the pleasure of the chairman. This was a problem because the selection process became quite political and was less dependent upon the skills of the mentor than it was upon political questions."

One of the authors implemented an HR mentoring program at a wireless communications company. Since one of the goals for the mentoring program was for the generalists to become better HR partners by increasing their knowledge of the business, it made perfect sense to pair up the generalists with mentors in the business. The pairing was made based on their field of interest and by the anticipated chemistry between the two. Once the partnerships were formed, the generalists were assigned business projects to complete with their mentors over a six- to nine-month period. At the end of the program, the generalists were expected to develop a business case. The development of this business case was required to "graduate" from the program. In this particular company's mentor program, the generalists were satisfied to be working with experts in the field with which they had chosen to become more knowledgeable. The mentors were flattered to have been selected and were pleased to share their knowledge. In a few of these cases, the generalists were paired up with their current business partner as a mentor. While this was a favorable move for some reasons, there were limitations around confidentiality and objectivity.

Choosing a mentor from outside the company may take more time and effort to identify but nonetheless has certain advantages. Keep in mind that it is a two-way selection. They need to decide whether there is value in it for them to mentor you. You are relying on the good will of a potential mentor, as they certainly have no obligation to participate. However, the pool to draw from externally is larger and more varied. If you are steering your career to another industry or venue, picking an outside mentor is more in keeping with your needs and you may get a better match than inside your company. Other advantages of having an outside mentor are additional confidentiality and objectivity.

Linda, an HR professional we spoke with, was having challenges communicating with her supervisor, as their management styles were very different. She realized she needed to improve the relationship or leave the company because there were limited opportunities there. She was definitely a candidate for an external mentor.

While it may take more time to bring an "outsider" up-to-speed on your environment, the advice you get will be more meaningful because it comes with the objectivity of being from another venue. Also, you have a greater assurance around confidentiality when your mentor comes from another company. Your potential feeling of "obligation" to an internal person who has been helpful to you is lifted when your choice is external. In summary, there are trade-offs in both instances. You need to make the decision of whether or not to go internal or external based on the specifics of your situation and the goals you have in mind for your mentoring relationship.

Finding the Right Mentor

The qualities of a good mentor will mean different things to different people. You may see it as based around comfort level and chemistry alone. However, there are some basics that you should look for. Here are some thoughts to keep in mind:

- Does the person you are considering fit the goals you have established for your relationship?
- Are they likely to be motivated to help? Are they genuinely motivated or just being polite?
- Do they have the time and will they be available based on your needs?
- Do they have the experience of being a mentor?

Experienced mentors are advantageous for obvious reasons, but if they are effective, they may have a following, and there could be a waiting list of folks wanting to engage their services. Since most mentors have their own careers, and they all have their own personal lives to attend to, trying to sign up with someone experienced with a good reputation can be challenging.

Here are some profiles of people who might be a good bet:

- Mr. X is retired, well financed and wants to keep his hand in the business world. While his health prevents him from engaging in a full-time job, he is willing to take on mentees to fill his part-time career goal.
- Ms. Z has a background in consumer package goods. She lost her product manager position a few months ago. With extra time on her hands, she is willing to take on mentees, especially in the consumer package goods industry.

Reaching Out for Help

Finding a mentor is not unlike finding a plumber, doctor, or other service. You want to ask around and cast the net, and see what names come back. You should use your network of industry contacts, consultants, academics, chambers of commerce, vendors, or HR associations for ideas. Mentors who are currently occupied may be able to give you some ideas. SCORE (Service Corps of Retired Executives) may be able to provide mentoring services. Also be sure to check with colleagues who have successful mentorships or have had them in the past.

SHRM has an online database that matches protégés with mentors. Robert LaGow, manager of Volunteer Relations for SHRM, oversees the program, which uses software developed by Triple Creek Associates. As of this writing, LaGow indicates that there are 1,450 mentors and 1,160 mentees. He describes the process as being similar to "E-Harmony," the online dating service where people are matched based on their needs.

Often, mentees become mentors and vice versa depending on the subject-matter expertise that is desired. Companies can forge these relationships cost effectively. By moving Baby Boomers into mentoring roles, companies can reduce the "brain drain" and ensure the company moves forward when key players leave. It is possible to connect with a local mentor or one in another state or city, and your data is protected ensuring confidentiality. LaGow says, "It is easy to set up mentoring programs, but hard to do them right. Think carefully about your goals and what you want out of it. Make sure there is buy-in on both sides."

Qualities of a Good Mentor
A good mentor will be:
- Engaging and easy to talk to, with good listening skills
- Supportive and compassionate when needed
- Objective and willing to push back to redirect you if needed
- Confidential and nonjudgmental

In making the determination of who would make a good mentor for you, be sure to talk to people who have had successful mentor relationships in the past. They should be able to tell you the qualities they valued. On the other side of the equation, it is equally important to find out about the relationships that were not successful so you can learn about potential pitfalls.

If, for example, one of the goals of your relationship is to develop a more strategic approach to your job, and you are missing those opportunities, a good mentor will identify the issue and bring it to the forefront in your discussions. A good mentor will pick up on patterns of behavior they have observed and reflect these back to you. For example, if you have a pattern of paying more attention to the transactional duties of your job while ignoring the opportunity to build relationships with director-level clients, this needs to be pointed out to you. A mentor needs to remind you about the goals you have established and continue to debrief you on the direction you have chosen. You need to be comfortable talking to your mentor openly and honestly. You also need to know that what you say will be held in strictest confidence, and that feedback will be given to you in a constructive and nonjudgmental way.

Linda Boatwright managed mentor programs for GE Aircraft Engine and Delta Airlines. She defined a good mentor as one who genuinely wants to be a mentor and is not doing it for political or career advancement reasons. They must enjoy the coaching and advisory role required of mentors and, most importantly, they must believe and live the bond of confidentiality.

Joe Martucci says, "They must take and have the time to spend with the mentee, but also need to avoid becoming a crutch for the individual. The primary role of the mentor is to be an intermediary and advisor. It is somewhat delicate as it requires a great deal of sound judgment."

Steve Gray, vice president, general manager, for AT&T Mobility, says, "good mentors have a genuine appeal. They have the maturity, seasoning, and life experiences to qualify. They must instill trust in the protégé, be objective and reflective."

A Two-Way Street

The relationship cuts both ways. The trust needs to be there for you to speak out or push back if you believe the mentor is recommending things that are not in your best interests. For example, if the mentor keeps cancelling the meetings that you have set up, you should confront him or her in a constructive way to express your disappointment. If that is going to jeopardize the relationship, so be it. Perhaps it wasn't healthy in the first place. Some may be intimidated by the level or stature of the mentor and give more latitude than normal. Also, it is common to feel hesitant about confronting the mentor, as the mentor is performing on a non-fee basis. However, business leaders want and expect to give back to the community on a pro-bono basis, and serving as a mentor may be one way they do it. If both are not in synch, the relationship doesn't benefit either party, and both parties are best served to repair or disband the relationship. It may take a few attempts to get a mentor with whom you feel comfortable and who can help you to achieve your goals. To minimize the time and effort expended, it is better to call the relationship to a halt if it is not working for either half.

Avoiding the Pitfalls

To avoid having to face a failed mentoring relationship, there are steps you can take to redirect the partnership.

- Interview potential candidates to determine the fit. Remember, potential mentors are also interviewing you.

- Set clear expectations. Talk about what you want to accomplish with the relationship and describe what things would be happening if the relationship were successful.

- Determine a time frame and benchmarks. As you consider mentors, weigh the amount of time they have to give against what you expect your needs will be. Perhaps if you have a very narrow area of need (i.e., wanting to learn about the potential of working with HR outsourcers) and your mentor knows a great deal about this topic, you may be able to get the help you need in a short amount of time. It may be a case of the mentor pointing you in the right direction or connecting you to their personal contacts who would be in the position to help you. You will need to gauge if a short amount of time with a great mentor means more to you than extended time with an average mentor.

Martucci adds: "Some mentors aren't suited to the role, particularly those who are dogmatic or controlling in their managerial approach. This quite frankly applies to both mentors and mentees."

Linda Boatwright described a mentoring relationship established with a high-level executive at GE. She says,

> *The relationship was flawed. The mentor and mentee had little in common. There needs to be a common base of interest ... It can be as simple as the love of music or an interest in learning how to play tennis ... it doesn't need to be career-focused.*

In this situation, the HR exec and her mentor were honest with each other in admitting that they didn't have a good match. They decided to disband the relationship and move on, as it was not benefiting either side.

The steps for approaching a mentor are similar to those for introducing yourself to a networking contact (see Chapter 6). Mentors may actually have been a networking contact. If you have a common contact that brought you together, you will have a better chance of making a successful connection. For example, "I understand you made a successful transition from Human Resources to a general management role. As I get close to finishing my MBA, I am giving more thought to a similar transition and Carl Johnson thought you would be an excellent person to talk to." A personal touch works best. You might send them an e-mail first to let them know generally what you are looking for and then follow up with a phone call asking to meet with them.

The mentor may contact people you both know to find out more about you and whether you would be a good bet as a protégé. He or she may or may not ask to see your resume, work samples, and performance reviews. One mentor we spoke to decided to turn down a request for a mentorship after he found out that the person requesting the mentorship did not have a good track record of follow through and with meeting commitments.

The best conditions are for you and your mentor to meet face-to-face. However, this may not be practical in light of busy schedules and different geographies. If needed, try to establish a mix of face-to-face and telephone meetings. In-person meetings would be most important as you are beginning your relationship. The more specific you can be about the format for your meetings and mutual expectations, the more likely your relationship will be successful. Some mentorships fail because the parties have not discussed what the mentorship activities will look like. Will there be projects or assignments, informal conversation, or a mix? Be aware that if the structure is too informal, progress towards the agreed upon goals may be impeded. After you agree on how your relationship will work, it is suggested that you consider a "contract" of understanding that you both sign and regularly review. The document can be very informal and nothing more than an e-mail confirming what you have discussed.

Martucci adds:

> *I am a big fan of timetables, routine reporting, and scheduled meetings and follow-up calls from the program administrators to the participants. You have to terminate the relationship and reassign where necessary. This can be embarrassing politically, so it is something of a hot potato.*

Boatwright says,

> *We developed and required mentors and mentees to sign a contract that included a program overview, objectives and guidelines, and time commitment to the partnership. We established quarterly group meetings to celebrate and discuss the program's effectiveness.*

A written agreement will add an element of commitment to your relationship, and you will have the basis to go back and review your progress against the established goals. It will help to keep the relationship on track. Your agreement should also include a statement about confidentiality. In considering the form of commitment, be sensitive to the style of your mentor, who may be informal and may not react well to formalizing your agreement. You and your mentor need to design the "program" that will fit your mutual needs. There is no "cookie cutter" approach to fit all. As you work through the process with your mentor to get your relationship established, you will learn a lot about each other that will serve you well as you embark upon your relationship.

Other Points about Mentors

Is one mentor enough? The response depends upon your needs. You may need one mentor to fit a specific need, but then want another mentor for broader career goals. For example, one of the authors established a mentor program for director-level sales executives. Each director was paired up with a counterpart in a different sales channel. Under this program, if a mentee's role involved selling to national retailers, he or she might have been set up with an executive who has responsibility for tele-sales. These pairings were developed to encourage cross-pollination between channels and to prepare executives to rotate to another channel in the future. Ideally the up-and-coming stars were being groomed to assume a broad-based sales management role in the future. However, while these mentor relationships were helpful in gaining knowledge and experience about a specific sales channel, participants may not have received general career guidance due to the targeted nature of the relationship. In that case, an executive may have opted to engage a second, more generalized, career mentor.

Dianne Sanchez, founder and principal of DAS Consulting, says that having more than one mentor is useful. For example, you could have one mentor for HR issues, and another for challenges related to the line business. You may have a third for your personal financial concerns.

Boatwright doesn't entirely agree,

> *I am of the belief that "quality" is better than "quantity" and to that end, I have not participated in successful mentoring programs where mentees had multiple mentors. I believe that the workplace is so demanding, especially in today's climate, that a solid one-on-one mentor relationship is far better than multiple ones that are haphazardly managed.*

Personal Board of Directors

If you start thinking about yourself as the CEO of your own company where you are the product, Erin Abrams recommends that you:

Create your own personal board of directors. Throughout your life, enlist people who inspire you, believe in you, and support your vision. Appoint them to your personal board of directors and make them hold you accountable to your vision for your own career and your own life.[4]

The board can include people from different walks of life, different communications styles, and different subject-matter expertise. For example, you might want to include a financial planner who can advise on the financial impact of your career plans. The Master Mind Alliance gives the following advice:

Consider the roles each person on your board will play. Consider having an entrepreneur along with a clarifier who asks clear questions, a connector who leads you to other people, a challenger who helps you act boldly, and a wise elder or sage. You want to draw upon the wisdom of people with diverse perspectives who think differently than you do.[5]

 Final Thoughts

- Developing relationships with mentors and coaches can provide a lifelong benefit to you in your professional and personal life.
- HR professionals will need to work harder at developing these relationships for themselves because typically these activities were reserved for their clients.
- HR professionals have special needs around mentorship due to confidentiality and other factors.

Packing
Your Suitcase

Rochelle has worked in Human Resources for six years and has a bachelor's degree in business with a concentration in Human Resources. She works as an assistant HR manager handling mostly recruiting and training. She has ambitions to move into a high-level HR generalist management job someday and has been looking for ways to get experience with her current company. She's pretty sure she needs more education but not sure if she should pursue another degree or try and get experience somehow in other areas. She's even thought about getting some kind of certification.

What educational background do you need to be successful as you grow your HR career? There are hundreds of undergraduate- and graduate-level programs offering concentrations or majors in HR management. In addition, there are many programs that offer a master's degree in HRM. These numbers may imply that a degree in Human Resources is necessary for your success. They also indicate that you have choices.

Certainly, if you expect to move up the organization ladder, a college degree is essential and will likely become more important that it be in Human Resources if you want to grow and stay in Human Resources.

If your goal is to become a manager, director, or the CEO or another C-Suite position, you should consider advanced or multiple degrees in business disciplines. The C-Suite has been and continues to be mostly white and male.[1] The C-Suite includes a company's chairman/CEO and executives such as the chief operating officer (COO) and chief financial officer (CFO).

IMD reports that just 45 percent of female executive committee members hold an MBA or business school degree, compared to 87 percent of their male counterparts. Similar disparities exist for other educational qualifications, such as advanced technical degrees, law and medical degrees, and Ph.Ds.[2]

This chapter will first look at how to determine your current areas of strengths and weaknesses. Then we will look at formal and informal ways to get the education and training you need to move forward. Finally, we will again provide examples of diverse educational backgrounds that have helped HR professionals move along in their careers.

What Do You Know?

Professional Certification

Taking courses and tests to qualify for professional certifications can be a good way to evaluate your knowledge. In addition to helping you assess yourself, passing the exam and getting the certifications gives you some measure of credibility. There are a number of organizations that provide these certifications.

The HR Policy Association represents the senior HR executives of more than 200 major U.S. corporations. It believes strongly that labor relations is a core competency that every HR professional should hold. To emphasize this viewpoint, they established the Labor Relations Professional Certification Program (HR Policy Association/LRP) to train and certify HR professionals in the most critical aspects of labor relations.

In recognition of the need to encourage excellence in public-sector Human Resources, to promote continuous learning, and develop the next generation of leaders, the International Public Management Association for Human Resources (IPMA-HR) offers two separate certification programs for the public HR community: IPMA-Certified Professional (IPMA-CP) and IPMA-Certified Specialist (IPMA-CS).

Certified Compensation Professional (or CCP) signifies a mark of expertise and excellence in all areas of compensation throughout the Human Resources and global rewards community. The CCP designation requires a passing score on nine examinations. There is no time limit for completion of these requirements, but periodic recertification is necessary to maintain current status of the CCP designation.

Certified Benefits Professional (CBP), a standard since 1976, and the Certified Compensation Professional (CCP) are designations known throughout the rewards community as a mark of expertise and excellence in all areas of compensation, according to the International Foundation of Employee Benefit Plans.

Work-Life Certified Professional (WLCP®) is designed to meet the growing need to develop strategies and implement effective work-life programs to improve an organization's bottom line and the lives of their employees. The new Work-Life Certified Professional designation includes four exams. The new designation is based on a body of knowledge that supports a comprehensive understanding of work-life effectiveness.

The Global Remuneration Professional (GRP) designation provides a foundation of compensation and total rewards knowledge spanning across borders.

The CPLP™ competency testing process requires candidates to pass both a knowledge exam and a work product assessment. The knowledge exam has 150 multiple choice questions covering nine areas. The work product assessment requires a sample of recent project work and essay responses. The work product must pertain to one of the following areas: Designing Learning, Delivering Training, Improving Human Performance, Measuring and Evaluating, Facilitating Organizational Change and Managing the Learning Function.

If you don't have a PHR, SPHR, or GPHR certification, it may be a good place to start. These certifications, as well as specific PHR-CA and SPHR-CA certifications for California, were established by the HR Certification Institute, an affiliate of the Society for Human Resource Management (SHRM), which represents more than 250,000 HR professionals (as of 2009). The exams that lead to certification evaluate your understanding of the HR Certification Institute defined Body of HR Knowledge. Currently, the functional areas are: Strategic Management; Workforce Planning and Employment; Total Rewards; Employee and Labor Relations; and Risk Management.

In our experience, professionals who have these certifications are perceived to be better qualified by the clients they serve. They may be viewed like a CPAs and other standard certifications in other fields. Based on our review of job postings, it is becoming more prevalent for HR certifications to be requested in listing qualifications for HR jobs. Roughly one-half of business leaders see differences between certified and noncertified HR professionals in terms of motivation, knowledge of the HR field, and performance.[3] Nearly three-quarters of business leaders believe that certified HR professionals inspire greater trust and confidence from business colleagues than do noncertified HR co-workers.

The exams (with the exception of the GPHR) test for generalist knowledge, so they may be a great jumping-off point for you if you've only been exposed to one or two functional areas and you want to move toward a more generalist future job. Pre-testing study materials are typically available through sponsoring organizations and test-prep publishers. These resources are an excellent way to take sample exams to get a handle on how the exams are structured and your level of knowledge without taking the final test or investing more time and money.

Taking a preparation course facilitated by an instructor is also a method for evaluating your knowledge levels along with potentially increasing that knowledge. Courses are offered through a network of colleges and universities. There are even some online offerings for the prep courses, and some vendors offer corporate training programs.

Though using the exams to evaluate your knowledge may not be an inexpensive method, it will give you a good picture of what you know.

Other Certifications

In addition to HR-related certifications, there are many industry-specific certification programs that may help you evaluate your knowledge if you want to target a position in one of them. Certifications in IT, for example, include those that point to expertise in particular software. In manufacturing, there are certifications in process management and efficiency like "lean techniques." If you have an interest in these areas or industries, we suggest that you do some Internet research.

Other Assessments

Assessment Centers

Professional assessment centers can be used to determine your cognitive skills (learning potential, your job-related behavioral traits), personal work style, personality, and your interests. Though often used by organizations to evaluate candidates for employment or for formal internal development programs, most are accessible to individuals. Fees for these services vary from a few hundred dollars to thousands of dollars.

According to Jim Hazen, a consultant in the assessment field, successful professionals in any field exhibit five traits:
1. Potential — they have the ability to do the job;
2. Personal Goals — their goals match those of the organization;
3. Positive Perception — others see them as doing the job well or see them as leaders;
4. Personality — their personality fits the requirements of the job; and
5. Performance — they actually do the work.[4]

Assessments, according to Hazen, help you to see yourself and your potential so that you can pursue the best job or career path.

When selecting a center or a service, it is important to make sure that the tests they are using are valid and reliable, and that the organization has some knowledge of HR competencies and skills.

The type of assessment that is used is important. It is generally acknowledged that "normative" assessments are better than "ipsative" assessments. The former compares an individual against a large number of similar-level individuals, while the latter evaluates self-perception.

Ipsative assessments include tools like DISC and many offshoots, which are based on William Moulton Marsten's 1938 work on how blood pressure could be used for lie detectors. Popular instruments like the Myers-Briggs Type Indicator, based on the marriage counseling tool created in the 1940s by Katherine Cook Briggs and Isabel Briggs Myers, are also ipsative in that they depend on how you view yourself. These can be highly useful when doing team-building activities but may not help as much for career analysis.

According to Hazen, these tools can be problematic when you are trying to be objective in evaluating yourself. It is better to use instruments that compare you with large numbers of individuals in the general population, and that focus on job success factors.

If your company uses these tools for development or selection, be sure to tap into this resource. If not, you may be able to access good evaluation tools through online resources. Most instruments today are delivered online and provide quick results. Using the services of an assessment center, though it involves some cost, also gives you the support of professional interpretation.

These assessments can help you determine your strengths and weaknesses, and how you might use your stronger areas and apply them to your career plans. They can also help you determine if a particular career path is right for you.

For example, you might want to become a benefits specialist because you see a future opportunity in your current organization. You may have provided benefits information to employees, and you may have assisted them in solving problems with insurance companies. On taking an assessment, however, you discover that your profile shows a low level of numerical reasoning, a crucial area for dealing with the many math calculations involved in benefits management.

This information may give you several options: don't pursue a path that may lead to failure and stress; look for a different type of job in benefits, maybe in another organization where you can specialize in the communication aspects;

get some specialized tutoring or training to help you with the math; or look for online tools that do the math analysis for you. Or is it possible that the benefits field is not for you?

Services provided by assessment centers may include testing, interviews, feedback sessions, reports, and recommendations for development.

Online Assessments

There are a number of quality online assessment tools available that are less costly and may involve less of a time commitment. The value of these is that you can plan around your schedule. Drawbacks may include less customized or personal feedback and discussion.

Depending on your own comfort level with using a computer, and the technical set up or technical requirements, you may have limits in using online assessments. In addition, if you don't have access to a private connection or space, it may be awkward to spend time taking the assessments.

Feedback from Others

One of the best ways to assess yourself is by asking for feedback from others. A 360-degree feedback assessment can yield lots of valuable information from co-workers, subordinates, and superiors. The challenge, however, in doing this kind of assessment is that people may be less likely to be honest in their feedback. As an HR professional, you do, like it or not, represent the management of the organization, and this may color the feedback results. Career offices may be able to administer these assessments for you; some are included online. If you take the test online, it is convenient and confidential. However, you will need to find a certified professional to interpret the results.

In addition, you may be looking to grow your career in a direction that your current organization can't provide. For example, if your goal is a higher-level management position in Human Resources, but your current job is the top position, how do you explain the 360-degree to your non-HR boss without telegraphing the potential that you might want to leave? In a perfect world, all bosses would want what's best for their employees, but we know this is not a perfect world. You have several options, including working with your boss, to "grow" opportunities within the company.

You can also ask for feedback from peers, mentors, and others if you have a good network outside the organization. If you are actively involved with a community, volunteer, or professional organization, you may be able to get feedback on your skills through those contacts.

You can also "assess" your skills by trying them out in less risky environments. By seeking and accepting leadership roles in organizations you can determine what you know about leadership and management, and what you still need to learn.

Leadership roles in local and national HR associations offer an opportunity to learn more about what it takes to lead and can help you determine where your strengths and weaknesses are without risking an employment situation.

One HR professional we interviewed learned about the importance of effective delegation. As president of her local HR association chapter, she was focused on growing membership, strategic planning, branding, and public relations. Unfortunately, she was not paying close enough attention to chapter finances. She had limited financial management experience and assumed that the treasurer and executive director had everything under control. However, this was not the case. The chapter lost money that year. Fortunately, they had lots of money in reserves, and she did grow the membership, which brought in increased revenues the following year. The experience led to her looking for more professional development courses in financial management. She also learned about the value of good delegation techniques that proved very important in later management positions.

Formal Education Programs

Changes in the business environment, including globalization, technology development, and shifting demographics have pushed the importance of formal education in Human Resources.

Many of the current mature HR professionals began their careers with degrees as varied as education, psychology, and accounting, or, in some cases, business.

Ommy Strauch, founder of Ommy Strauch and Associates and a past chair of SHRM, says that she realized early on that her bachelor s degree in Business was not enough if she wanted to advance in Human Resources, so she returned to school to get an advanced degree. She advises HR professionals to always keep in sight of their career goals and be willing to do whatever it takes, including paying their dues in the necessary work, to learn and grow as professionals.

Formal education has become more significant, and it is unlikely that you will be able to advance your career without having an education. Table 8.1 offers some insights related to various degrees.

Table 8.1

Type of Degree You Have	Possible Additional Education	Evaluate
Undergraduate degree outside of Human Resources	Advanced degree in Human Resources	• What is my career goal? • Will I be overeducated and inexperienced? • What is respected in my organization, industry, global culture?
No degree	Undergraduate degree in Human Resources	• Do I have management interest and potential? • What is important in my career objective?
Undergraduate degree in Human Resources	Advanced degree in Human Resources or another field	• Do I want to advance in Human Resources? • Do I want to move toward some other management area? • Do I need more knowledge in a particular career field or industry? • What is respected in my organization, industry, global culture?

Be clear about your goals for getting the degree. Don't set yourself up for unrealistic expectations, i.e. automatic promotion.

SHRM published a set of HR Curriculum Templates after studies revealed that college programs were inconsistent in what they offered. Though the templates are not meant to be requirements for college programs, they may be helpful for you in evaluating programs. They may also help you assess your own strengths or weaknesses to bolster your career plan development.[5]

When looking at HR formal education programs, you should examine key factors:

• What classes are offered and how do they relate to your career goals?
• How often are the core classes offered?
• What kinds of electives are offered?
• Is there flexibility as to location and methodology (bricks and mortar vs. online)?
• How does the program/curriculum fit with your available time?

- What is the success rate of students in the program and graduates?
- How many students start the program and how many finish?
- What is the employment rate of graduates?
- Where are graduates employed? How aggressive is the institution's placement department?
- Does the program have any formal alliances with HR associations?
- What are the full costs of the program (including tuition, books, student fees, room and board, if relevant, transportation, etc.)?
- What are the requirements for being accepted into the program?
- Is there an active Career Placement Office?

Look, too, at the instructors in the programs. Do they have real-world experience in Human Resources and business? Career academics are critical to any program, but they should still be involved with research, and working with businesses to do that research. Most programs provide detailed online biographies and/or curriculum vita or resumes of their faculty; look for professional experience, frequency of nonacademic publications, presentations to professional organizations, and so on.

Does the program you are considering require some practical experience activities or research projects that you can use to tie into your everyday work?

One HR professional we interviewed was able to transition into a full-time HR management position from a graduate student internship by creating a capstone project that involved researching and developing a corporate university for the company. Upon graduation, the organization put her into a position to manage the program.

Find out about the reputations of various schools in your area by talking to other HR professionals. Does your organization, or your target organization, or career path prefer certain degree programs?

Finally, consider taking advantage of any tuition assistance programs available to you. Though formal education is an investment in your future, it can be expensive. Sources of help could include your current organization or some other organization where you might go. Also look for scholarships. Professional organizations often offer scholarships. There are books and online sources for and about scholarships.

Other HR-Related Degree Programs

Some schools don't offer a degree with an HR title but may offer a business degree with an HR concentration. Programs may be on both the undergraduate and graduate levels. If you want to consider these programs, there should be at least four or five electives to choose from in Human Resources. Courses like Legal Aspects of HR Management, Labor Economics, Change Leadership, Training and Development, Organizational Development, or Compensation and Benefits are some that may be typical in business schools.

Degrees are also available in labor relations or organizational development. These are usually at the graduate level and may focus more strongly on a particular aspect of the HR world. Consider whether they support the direction you want to go. Consider also whether there are job opportunities in these areas.

Certificate Programs

The term "certificate" means many things. Some colleges offer specialized courses in which you receive a certificate upon successful completion, rather than a diploma. It is not the same thing as a "certification" in Human Resources or a related field; rather, it is an abbreviated program for which the student receives a certificate upon successful completion. These programs may be credit or noncredit programs, and may be graduate level or continuing professional development. They are appealing to working professionals since they usually provide focused education in critical areas. They involve less time commitment and often may be used in the future as transfer credits for full-degree programs.

Again, before signing up for any of these programs, consider asking the same questions outlined above. Make sure that the education you receive will support your career plans and help you fill in any gaps.

Noncredit certificate programs can be helpful too, particularly if you already have a degree, especially a master's degree, and you want more knowledge or need to develop skills in a particular area. These programs may be less expensive and usually don't have the same load of work as a credit program might have.

Again, don't forget to ask about what is covered, who is teaching, and any data they have on success rates. Also, consider those courses affiliated with recognized business schools or reputable organizations that meet accreditation or some formal standards. Remember, you can get a "medical" degree or become an "online" minister, but we'd be unlikely to ask you to treat our illnesses or officiate at our kid's weddings!

Conferences and Workshops

Local organizations, HR associations and professional organizations, law firms, local chambers of commerce, other membership and business associations, and HR product suppliers offer nonaccredited, but valuable and timely education programs and workshops that can help with your professional development. The key is determining what information or skills you need, and evaluating the program to determine its fit for you.

Other sources for education include state agencies or federally sponsored programs. If you are considering moving into a career as an HR consultant (starting your own business), for example, you will need to know how to write a business plan. Local colleges and universities may have programs funded under the U.S. Small Business Administration through state agencies that are free or relatively affordable.

Professional Development within Your Organization

Many larger organizations have their own corporate universities that offer professional development programs. They may not seem like topics that you would consider HR functions, but programs on financial management, green initiatives, project management, and even production efficiencies like quality management systems may help you develop in the direction you want to go with your career.

If you are concerned about your boss wondering why you want to learn about production when it is not part of your job, you should be prepared with a good argument. For example: "If I understand what is needed in the production area, I can better determine and plan for appropriate recruiting strategies. Besides, I'll get to know the production people better and they may be more willing to partner with HR."

How You Learn

What is your learning style? It is generally accepted that we all learn in three ways: using auditory information, visual data, or kinesthetically by manipulating things. Usually we have a more dominant style. By knowing what your dominant style is, you can pick the best learning method or at least adapt the available method to suit your style.

You may already be aware of your style by thinking back on the best experiences you have had. Did you do well in college lecture classes or were you better when there were lots of visuals used in the instruction? Did you learn from reading, which is both auditory and visual? Do you do best when you can work with actual examples or handle and manipulate things (kinesthetic)?

A learning styles assessment might be available from an assessment center.

Though good professional development programs try to include all three, you may best learn from selecting ones that fit your style. For example, some people learn facts best by listening and could use podcasts or recorded media.

Others do better with face-to-face classes where they can discuss materials and argue points verbally.

What Makes a Good Program?

The quality of a program can be determined by reviewing the content, objectives, previous reviews, and references from your peers. Picking a good development program is at least as important as making a major purchase.

It's important to be aware of the basic difference between a conference workshop and a course or educational program that takes a larger time commitment.

Workshops at a conference may be limited to a focused coverage of a small part of a topic or a brief coverage of the most important points. This is not to say that attending conferences is not valuable for your professional development, but you should evaluate the depth of knowledge you need before choosing a program.

Education through Experience

Another internal-development method is to learn through participation on internal teams and task groups, or requesting job-rotation assignments or cross-training.

Within HR, rotation and cross-training are usually best approached as a hedge against loss if others within the department are absent or leave.

Getting involved outside of Human Resources may be trickier. You may need to work at providing rationale — for not only your boss but for the employees in other departments — for including an HR person on the team. HR personnel may be seen as intruders and may even be thought to be "spying." One way to overcome this resistance is to target a project or problem that is shared across functions and "suggest" that a task group be established. In doing this, you help other managers know that you care about the things they care about. The problem should be something that you can learn from but which you can contribute some expertise in solving. This can enhance visibility and demonstrate your willingness to learn more about business. Evidence from various studies has revealed that business managers want Human Resources to understand business to better provide the support and services they need.

One of the authors was able to do this when she wanted to learn more about work within one of her organization's divisions. The division provided services to members, including career development resources. She approached the division about working together to set up an on-site career fair at a conference the division sponsored. A cross-functional team was formed, and she was able to provide good input in how to structure the fair and was also able to provide ideas for education programs for the members on how to interview and write resumes.

At the same time, she learned more about how the division functioned and about the members of the organization. She later applied for a position with that division as part of her career plan.

What if you can't get enough of the right kind of experience within your organization? What if there is a lack of support and you can't sell your ideas?

Volunteering

Let's say you work for a small- to mid-sized organization where you are responsible for staffing and training. You have determined that you want to move into HR management using your 10 years of experience. Your current boss' job is the only one at that level, and it is clear that she is not planning on leaving the position in the near future. In analyzing your skills, you realize you need more management know-how and experience to get a management job but you can't get it at work. What do you do?

This is the scenario one of the authors found herself in at one point in her career. She tried to apply for management jobs but was told she didn't have enough experience, which was a point she couldn't argue. The answer came in an opportunity to earn management experience through her volunteer work as a SHRM chapter leader. She started working as a committee member and moved up to a chairperson on several committees. As she developed her leadership skills, including some opportunities to attend SHRM Leadership programs, she was recognized as having the potential to be a chapter officer.

She moved through the ranks, getting experience in leading and motivating volunteers, managing programs, doing strategic planning for the chapter, and managing financials. She did make some mistakes, but the chapter didn't fold as a result of any of them.

Her skills and network grew, as did her confidence in her ability to be a leader. Finally, after her year as president of the chapter, she was able to secure a director of Human Resources position in another organization.

Volunteer work doesn't have to be in a SHRM chapter, but the networks the author developed there certainly led to further career success.

Volunteer work for a social service organization or an arts organization can also help you build your skills. Most organizations are looking for people with an understanding of Human Resources to contribute that assistance. Positions on boards of directors of these organizations can help you develop great skills. Examples of organizations that might help you find opportunities include Boards-by-Design at Duquesne University in Pittsburgh that links people with nonprofit boards, or the Board of Directors Network in Georgia, which is a part of The Inter-Organization Network (ION), an organization that promotes getting women on boards.

Mentorships

Mentorships can help you develop skills in both "directions." Being a mentor can help you to develop your coaching skills. Having a mentor can give you opportunities to learn more about the areas in which your mentor is an expert. See Chapter 7 for more information.

 Final Thoughts

- Learning and development takes many forms. Consider what is the best fit for you and your needs.
- Don't invest in additional education before determining if there is a potential return on the investment for your career path.
- Know what you need before seeking development, and don't just depend on your self-perceptions.
- Being a lifelong learner is the key to success in any field, and in Human Resources it may be the difference between career success and failure.

Embarking
on the Trip

Dennis has been working on his career planning. He's been the HR manager in a small company for a dozen years. He understands that, due to the size of the company, he has no place to move up if he wants to advance in Human Resources. He's done all of his prep work, including getting his professional certifications in Human Resources (he's an SPHR) and in compensation management, his target career path. He's decided that it is now time to look for a new job. But, he's wondering where best to start? It's been a long time since he sat on the other side of the desk.

Directions Drive Your Actions

If you determined your career goals, evaluated the options in your current organization, and closed the gaps in knowledge, competencies, and skills, you may be ready to make a job transition.

You might be looking to move up, backwards, or sideways in your career. Any of these directions will help you move forward in your career plan.

Whether you are taking a step toward that higher-level job in Human Resources or another business area, planning your "retirement" career, seeking a temporary role to keep your life in balance, or simply checking your value in the job market, you will be looking for a job.

Where you look will be driven by your ultimate goal, but how you look will involve some or all of the actions suggested in this chapter.

Finding a Job *Is* a Job

A non-HR professional we spoke with questioned why we would need to have a chapter devoted to the job search. "After all," he said, "I thought all HR people knew how to do a job search."

Much like the doctor without band-aids in his house or the shoemaker whose kids don't have shoes, many of us know how to find people but don't know how to *market ourselves*. In addition, those of us who do not do recruiting as a major part of our jobs (or those of us who have not done it recently) may not know what is going on in the field.

It appears to us that HR professionals often just expect people to notice how good they are and offer them the next job. More than 35 percent of HR professionals surveyed in 2007 indicate they got their current jobs through internal promotion or transfer.[1] This suggests to us that HR professionals historically have not done personal strategy and planning to move up the career ladder and instead may end up in positions by default.

The entire philosophy of this book is that your career is entirely in your hands, and if you are proactive about making good moves and competent, then you are more likely to get your dream job.

Being in Human Resources may mean that there is less support available in your own organization or more risk if you share your ambitions with others in your organization, particularly if you are looking to leave.

Plan Your Time

The first step is to determine how much time you will spend on your search. The rule of thumb is that for every $10,000 of salary you want to make, add one month to your search time (e.g., a $50,000 salary = five months). This is true if you are spending 30-40 hours a week on search activities, and if it is an average economy and job market, and if you have realistic goals.

In an HR role, we often find ourselves struggling to just keep up with the daily grind. If you are in a functional role, or in a 24/7 or international organization, you may be working long hours to serve the needs of your internal clients. But if you want to develop your career, you *must* make time to work on your action plans.

If you are employed full-time and have a personal life you want to keep, then be prepared for the search to take a long time. On the other hand, if your career developing strategies are an ongoing exercise and not just because you suddenly need a job, then many of the "start-up" activities are already in place.

It probably goes without saying that you should not spend time looking for a new job while working at your current job, unless there is a way to tie in current work with your job or that it is part of some downsizing/restructuring "benefit."

Make a Place and Assemble Your Documents and Tools

Preparing a functional work area will help in a professional execution of your career strategies. After setting aside a time frame, you should set up a place to work on your job search. You may be able to work in your office if this is an open search or you are able to use the company equipment during off hours. Keep in mind, though, that using company equipment could put you at risk of someone finding out you are looking for a job.

Next, you want to make sure you have the information documents you need. Here's a checklist:

- Updated resume, including several versions to emphasize strengths or industries you might be applying to
- Spreadsheet or other document where you can record data on your job search activity
- Your HR Travel Itinerary (see Chapter 4 and Appendix)
- Directory of your current network contacts
- Back-up documents such as copies of diplomas, certification documents
- Documents related to recognition or awards or accomplishments
- List of your professional references (pre-confirm their willingness to serve as good references)
- Detailed list of former jobs, including supervisor's names and full contact information
- Business cards. If you are unemployed, this is a critical item, as it conveys you are serious and makes you look professional. It is much easier for people to take away with them than a copy of your resume. Your card should include your name, contact information, and a "title" or list of titles that indicate your goal positions. If you have a good printer on your computer, you can buy blanks and print your own cards from your computer or you can have some printed at a local office store or print shop. Some web-based services even offer up to 250 free cards if you are willing to choose from a limited number of styles and you don't mind having their ads on the reverse side.

Resume or Bio Development

An HR professional should know how to prepare an effective resume for themselves or how to coach a client to do the same. A resume is an advertisement where you are the product. It should be a sound summary of what you have accomplished. It is not a statement of what you want to do. Career goals in resumes are currently not in vogue. Your career goals are better expressed in an interview or networking meeting.

Job hunters sometimes have more than one resume based on the industry or niche they are targeting. For example, someone who is willing to entertain a job in a corporate as well as a consulting environment may use two different resumes based upon the people they are talking to.

Based on the authors' experience, HR professionals turn out ineffective resumes. This could be from a lack of knowledge or a lack of practice. Those folks who have responsibilities for staffing are in the position to see plenty of resume examples that they can review or model. A resume is

---

Quick Tips for Resumes

- You should be able to tell the story in two pages.
- Most recent company should be listed first.
- If you've recently left a company, it is OK to show the dates as "to present" for a 90-day period provided you explain during the interview. After that period of time, show the month and year you left.
- Use plenty of white space, bulleting, bolding. Make it easy to read.
- These days, most resumes are transmitted electronically. You should have two versions of each version of your resume: a word processed format and a plain text format.
- Write in the third person. Full sentences are not needed in all cases.
- Describe your job in terms of accomplishments using quantifiable information.
- Avoid "job description" type activities.
- Resumes are evolutions: If you ask 100 people for feedback, you're bound to get 100 different opinions. Incorporate the best suggestions, but at some point you need to run with it and adjust along the way.
- For job dates, months are not needed other than the most recent job if you left mid-year.
- Write it yourself. By doing so you will be able to speak to the accomplishments with credibility and conviction during the interview.
- Save former copies of resumes. They can be helpful when you do updates, as well as good reminders of former experience for interview situations.
- A good resume can be developed and printed on your computer. Other than choosing high-quality, bonded paper, nothing fancy is needed.
- Gimmicky resumes, colored paper, and brochures won't play well in Human Resources.
- If your education (degree) was completed more than 10 years ago, don't list the dates of graduation. The information may reveal your age, and once a degree is 10 years or older, the fact that you got it is more important than when you got it.

simply a written statement of who you are and what you have accomplished professionally.

If your company does business with an outplacement company or other career services organizations, you might ask to see the materials given to employees or former employees who use these services.

You should always have a current resume on file for a search firm that contacts you unexpectedly with a hot opportunity. Another reason for keeping your resume up-to-date is that the passing of time plays games with our memories. When your boss asks you to submit a list of your accomplishments for the year to be used in the performance appraisal process, be sure to retain them in a dedicated computer or hard copy file, as these lists become the basis for excellent accomplishment statements in resumes, as well as talking points for job interviews.

What's a Bio?

A "bio" is different from a resume. It is a few paragraphs giving a broadbrush summary of your background, key accomplishments, and areas of expertise. It does not generally get into the detail about companies you worked for (other than the current), years worked, and specifics of what you did there. It might refer to the industries you've worked in. It should reflect your educational background.

Bios are generally requested as a way to introduce you if you will be presenting or training. You will generally be in the position to write your own bio. It is another marketing statement of who you are and what you have done. It is a great way to mold how you want people to remember you.

Job Search in the Electronic World

If you are to be successful, today's job-search strategies need to include the electronic communication components. Many of the recruiters and management professionals with whom you need to connect use electronic tools.

Establishing a page on a web site can also add to your job-search tools. Social networking sites may be helpful in spreading the word about what you have to offer.

Sites like Facebook will certainly link you to recruiters who use them but there may be a downside to using them if you include too much personal information. These sites do have some entries that are less than professional at times, and there is some concern about security and who actually owns your information once you post it on the site.

One site that is considered to be a professional/business networking site is LinkedIn. You may want to look at *Seven Days to Online Networking* for more ideas on using social networking sites.[2]

Before posting on any sites, carefully review any available information on access and audience, and make sure you are posting information that will make you look professional. Remember, too, that anything you post on the Internet, including personal blogs, may end up being viewed by anyone. Use a search engine on your own name to see what is already out there that someone else might see. Make every effort to change or resolve any "bad press" you come across by contacting the source or publishing a response or explanation.

Other Handy Information

Along with your updated resume, you should have any back-up and research data you gathered as you developed your career plan. Your resume will probably not include all of the details about past jobs, experience, and education, but that information will provide some good preparation material for interview time. If you have this information handy, it will also enable revisions of your resume for targeting specific positions.

In addition, you may want to make some notes on critical incidents in your career that might be good responses to behavioral-oriented questions at an interview. Interviewing tips are discussed later in this chapter.

Where to Start Looking

The most obvious places to look for positions are in your own organization's publications, as well as in publications such as journals and newspapers. You may work for a large company that posts jobs to all employees. Be aware that newspapers and print media have lost ground to electronic media as places to advertise jobs.

There are hundreds, maybe thousands, of web sites that companies use to post positions. The big job boards like Monster and CareerBuilder are certainly worth looking at for postings you might be interested in pursuing. Most require that you "register" with them, and few charge the job seeker. They enable you to set up job alerts after you input basic criteria for the kind of job you are looking for. Take care not to be overly reliant on these sites, as they attract thousands of applicants and the chances of receiving a call back are small.

There are smaller organizations that may have good positions you'd be interested in but they can't afford the big fees charged by the big boards. Check out sites sponsored by specific career-centered organizations like SHRM's HR Jobs or local chapter sites for a specific location. If you are considering a transition from Human Resources into another field, check sites for that field. For example, the American Society of Association Executives (ASAE) has listings of professional societies which represent hundreds of other careers. If you are looking for a position in a particular industry, say health care, you might find sites that target that industry like http://healthcarejobs.org/. Of course if you know the names of companies you are interested in, look at the employment opportunities/careers/jobs section of the company web site.

One way to search for job information that goes beyond the obvious entry "hr jobs in PA" on a web browser or search engine is to be aware of some specific Boolean search tools / language. Do you know that by creating a "string" in the search request you can narrow down the results you get? For example, if you are looking for an HR manager position in Pittsburgh, you might enter the following in the search field:

intitle:HR manager|inurl:HR manager (Pennsylvania|PA) (412|724)

What you are asking for here is any listing that has HR manager in either the title or the URL — the colon (:) indicates "look for this word or phrase"; the pipe (|), which can be found at the far right on your keyboard, usually above the backslash (\), is the symbol for the word "or." The space between "manager" and "(Pennsylvania|PA)" means "and." By asking for the state, either spelled out or the whole word, you narrow down the search again. Finally, the (412|724) are the telephone area codes for the Pittsburgh area. This will narrow the results from the 283,000 you get if you just enter "HR Manager Jobs Pittsburgh PA" to 8,920. If you add a minus sign (the symbol for "not") and a word like "consulting" (meaning "don't" include any listing with the word consulting in it), the results are lowered to 5,490. While this is still a large number, by using these tools you may be able to search more effectively for the jobs you would be interested in applying for.

The Hidden Jobs

As you may know, less than a third of jobs are "visible" or advertised publicly. The graphic below illustrates this point. It may actually be less than that when you consider various industries and careers. This means that if you plan to look for an opportunity to move forward in your plan, you need to do a lot of networking. It is only through networks that you will find out about jobs that are being filled using confidential searches, jobs that will be available tomorrow (so you can be ahead of the other candidates), and jobs that may not even exist yet but may be the result of someone meeting you and seeing the need for your unique skill set in their organization (see Figure 9.1).

We've covered the subject of networking skills in Chapter 6 — your networks can provide you with information, services, and advice as you function in your HR job. Here we are talking about using an even broader network to find jobs.

Figure 9.1 **Job Opportunities**

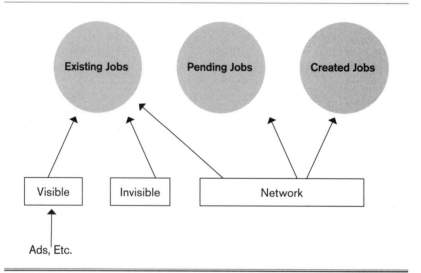

Who Should Be in Your Job Search Network?

When you are looking to make a transition, first consider your plan and make a list of anyone you already know who might be in your target industry or specialty. Next, add to that list anyone who might know someone in the target area.

This is one of those areas where people may hesitate, since we in Human Resources are expected to be the leaders of the loyalty within an organization. We may fear getting a bad rap if it is discovered that we are looking around.

There are several ways to deal with this issue. The first is to "come clean" to your boss and hope for support. It is possible that you will be pleasantly surprised by a positive reaction from your direct supervisor. He or she may even offer to help. However, if you are fairly sure that this would be a bad move, don't do it. You may have to take selected contacts you trust into your confidence and ask them for their help in your job search.

If you are unemployed, networking is a little more difficult but even more important. As you ascend the corporate career pyramid, who you know and the connections you make are critical in landing another opportunity. Conventional wisdom is that at least 60 percent of jobs are landed through a networking approach. Therefore, you should be spending an equivalent amount of your time engaged in networking activity, meaning several networking meetings or calls (one-on-one or group) per day.

The reality is that while most people are eager to help others going through career transition, they are not subject to the time urgency as those who are out of work. Then there is the blow to the ego that is part of losing a job. Advice to job seekers is to request network contact meetings for information (i.e., the company, industry, a particular subject area of interest), but not to ask for a job. Asking for a job puts your contact on the spot and makes them feel uncomfortable. Taking this approach is likely to end the discussion. It is clearly a more delicate discussion.

The key is to focus on uncovering the desired information or getting additional introductions to others who can help in similar ways. It is easier to get a networking meeting with someone if you can say that you were referred by a common contact as opposed to a "cold" call. Networking meetings should last about 30 minutes, unless the subject chooses to extend the length. Good recordkeeping and other tips mentioned below apply.

From your initial list of network sources, look at each and evaluate the level of confidence you have in their ability and willingness to help you while remaining reasonably confidential. This is where having HR peers can be a plus, since most of your networks know how to maintain confidences just by virtue of their profession.

Keep in mind that no matter how quiet you try and keep things, a secret told is no longer a secret, so there is always risk. But if you can't find available jobs, you will never progress. It is a fine line to walk.

Applying to jobs through job postings and job sites can often be like a "black hole," as you rarely get a response. Your application becomes one of hundreds that have to be reviewed. However, if a member of your network knows someone at the target company, that person can forward your resume directly to the hiring manager. This kind of "warm" introduction goes a long way in getting your resume to the top of the pile and increasing the probability of being called for an interview.

If you've got some good mentors, you certainly can use them to help connect you with available positions.

What If Networking Makes You Uneasy?

Some of the people in your network come to be there by chance. You may meet them through work or organizations you belong to, or through services you use like your insurance agent, etc. Keep in mind that everyone is a potential member of your network.

But though you may be able to talk to people effectively in the performance of your job, you may not be comfortable introducing yourself to a stranger in social situations. Some people have said that they feel uncomfortable because they feel guilty about their intent being to "use" the other person to get a contact or a job.

There are several things you can do to help yourself in these situations. One is by using your HR skill of interviewing. An HR professional we know once said that she overcomes her discomfort on meeting someone new by actually "interviewing" them. When she asks questions about their work, it makes people feel good because she is demonstrating an interest in them. This technique breaks the ice and helps establish a relationship.

If you are feeling guilty, keep in mind that any relationship should go both ways. The network you make may help you in developing your own career but you may then be able to be a source of information or contacts for the other individual. It's probably a good idea to make an offer of help when you thank the individual for their help.

Networking at Events

Any event may be an opportunity to network. Social events, professional organization meetings, and educational programs can generate career-advancement leads. Many local churches and organizations hold regular networking groups for job seekers. There are also groups that are dedicated to HR professionals. These groups take on more prominence during times of economic downturns. Be careful though, you don't want to be labeled as "the person who's looking for a job who no one wants to invite to a party." If you use good judgment about who you talk to, you can grow your opportunities.

Do some homework prior to an event to determine who will be in attendance and then plan on talking to those individuals who may be a good addition to your network.

Using Your Network

Using your network effectively means "working" it by communicating and requesting time to talk; being prepared for every meeting with an agenda; requesting times and dates for follow-up; and maintaining good records on all conversations.

Make sure you research the individual and the company as much as possible before requesting a networking meeting. It may be obvious that you can use the Internet to do this but don't forget that you can search for individuals as well as companies. If you expect them to be willing to help you, you want to demonstrate an interest in the individual and their company.

Always ask who else the individual might suggest you speak to, and make notes and follow up. It is also a good idea to ask the person you are speaking with how you might help them. Even if they can't think of anything at the time, it makes your relationship with them more balanced. In other words, it is not just about you. There are instances where your networking contact comes back to you some time later with something you can help them with. It might even be an opportunity to do some work for them, participate in a committee they are running, etc.

Leave a business card behind and, when appropriate, a resume.

Follow Up

People today are busy and they may not respond quickly. Being assertive, but tactful, and following up with your contacts is essential. You don't want to be a nag, but at the end of a networking conversation, if you ask, "When can I expect to hear back from you?" or "When may I check back with you?", you have a good reason to contact them again in their time frame. It is important to track this information using a spreadsheet or a calendar or Outlook or other electronic calendar.

Electronic Networking

We discussed having information posted on web sites and using social and business networking sites earlier. These can also be used to look for opportunities. Keep in mind that these networking sites are often more visible to the public. So if you are keeping your search quiet, it may be difficult to use them.

In a tight job market, many recruiters are searching these sites for the passive job hunter. Post your information or resume as part of your "profile" on these sites and you may get contacts.

People who are registered in a social network include those with and without jobs. It is a less intrusive place to communicate and may reduce the stress level that can be associated with networking. Also, if you want to meet a specific individual to help with your job search, you can use your network to identify contacts you have in common to get introductions to people you want to meet.

A Word about Interviews

If your specialty or experience is in staffing and recruiting, this information may be old news for you. But even if you are a skilled interviewer and you have read the information in Chapter 6 about "must-have skills," being on the other side of the desk involves a different skill set.

The purpose of an interview for both the interviewer and interviewee is to see if the job is a good fit. If you have a good interviewer, it should be a good experience where there is a sharing of information. As the interviewee, it may be possible to exert a level of control during the process, but only if you are well prepared.

Remember not to talk too much. Listening is as critical as talking in an interview. If you don't listen to the questions so that you can effectively answer them, you will not be successful.

HR professionals can take their "inside" knowledge of how companies recruit and use this information to their advantage in preparing for interviews where they are the candidate. If a company conducts good interviews, it becomes easy for the HR candidate to present his or her knowledge, skills, and accomplishments, *provided* he or she is prepared.

If an interviewer is not skilled at effective interviewing, you, as the candidate, will need to work harder to mold and shape the interview time to your benefit and to find the way to showcase your qualifications.

Preparation

Before the interview, gather information about the organization and the interviewer by using your researching skills discussed in Chapter 6. Some interviewers will form an important first impression about you based on how much preparation you did to learn about the company in advance.

Some sources:
- Internet:
  - » Company web page
  - » Search engine like Google, news articles, bio information, etc.
  - » Social networking links
- Call or e-mail network contacts that you have who might know the interviewer

- Library research — Dunn and Bradstreet, Hoovers, and other business directories

Data you should gather includes:
- Organization Mission, Vision, Values
- Traits and skills listed in any public job postings
- Company culture clues — how long have they been in business; where are they based (off-shore culture influences); what is going on in the industry group; private, public, family business type; any awards recognitions; community involvement initiatives
- Interviewer background information, education, and interests
- Reputation from those who have worked there; turnover trends

Don't over prepare to the point you find yourself telling them about their company. Rather, you want to be able to know enough to tailor your answers to questions to the organization's needs. In addition, when you demonstrate knowledge about the company, you show your interest in the job, the organization and the interviewer.

Practice interviewing. Even if you are a skilled professional in doing an interview, finding yourself on the other side of the desk can be disconcerting, so you want to make sure your come across confidently. Practicing with a peer or even a family member often works well. Even looking in the mirror can help you "see" how you are coming across.

Try to develop some expected questions or do some Internet research looking on sites like Monster or CareerBuilder, where there may be hints and tips for a list. Ask your HR peers who are recruiting specialists if they can share some questions.

Take advantage of technology to practice. One young man who was being coached by one of us used his PC camera to record his responses to interview questions. He could then play back the results and make improvements in his style. Video recording your practice and reviewing the results is also an option.

Watching interviews — even those that are not for employment — and critiquing the person being interviewed can help. Politicians and entertainers often do some of the best interviews, so you can learn from them.

Rehearse nonverbal gestures (such as placement of hands and legs, eye contact, and posture) in advance. Ideally, have an expert videotape you during a mock interview situation and provide a critique.

Prepare three to five questions that you will ask, given the opportunity. Remember that an interview is an exchange of information. Be prepared to use the interview as a tool to determine if the company and the job meet your personal requirements.

Consider accepting some interviews for jobs that you are not sure you want. Every time you do an interview, you gain experience, which will make you better the next time. In addition, you may discover that you are interested in the company or the job after visiting and learning more about them. You may also expand your network; if you make a good impression, they may think of you later for a job that is a better fit. Don't spend so much time doing this that you don't get your other "work" of job hunting done.

Types of Questions You Might Be Asked

Be prepared to share several accomplishment stories (situation, action, result) that you may be asked about directly or you may have to weave into your answers. The situations should correlate with accomplishments on your resume. They should also be based on a value proposition of what you did to impact the business and create value.

You are likely to experience several types of questions during the interview, and by thinking about them ahead of time you will think better on your feet.

1. Broad, general questions — these are intended to break the ice, or sometimes to probe for self-knowledge or creativity, or to understand what you think is important.

    Some examples:

    - How does this job fit into your career plans?
    - Where do you see yourself in five years?
    - Tell me something about yourself that I can't see on your resume.

2. Behavioral questions — these questions ask you to explain how you did something in the past and draw on your past experience.

    Some examples:

    - Tell me about a time when you had to deal with a difficult employee.
    - Describe the method you use to keep track when you find yourself juggling lots of jobs.

3. Demonstration questions — these give you an example or a problem and ask you how you would deal with it.
    Some examples:
    *   Outline how you would handle this situation: Your first day on the job your boss has a family crises and calls in to say she will be out for the next three weeks and you are in charge. Or: An employee comes to your office, closes the door, and starts crying.
        » Say that you get this job and your first assignment is to create a new benefits program, where would you start?

4. Trait questions — these asks you to identify something about yourself and your likes, dislikes, or needs.
    Some examples:
    *   If I gave you a magic wand and asked you to use it to get the ideal boss, what would that person be like?
    *   At your job at Company X, what do you find the most frustrating?

Be prepared to answer the question about what your strengths and areas for development are. You want to be candid but also tailor the answer to the needs of the job. There is no perfect candidate. A "weakness" could be that you need to acquire more knowledge or experience in a particular area, but that you have already researched ways to fill in a gap. You can also be prepared to turn a weakness into a strength. For example: "I may sometimes work too hard since I have a strong work ethic and I forget to make time to relax." Employers want people who are willing to work hard.

You can't anticipate every question, but if you think through and even practice answering questions with a buddy, you will be better prepared.

Situations

You might be involved in a group or panel interview, particularly if the job involves working with a group of managers or even board members. When responding to a group, you should generally address your answers to the person asking the questions and periodically make eye contact with the others in the group.

Interviews during a meal can be a challenge. Order something small or easy to eat so that you are not distracted from the questions by trying to neatly eat a plate of spaghetti or even a salad. And, of course, even if the interviewer orders an alcoholic beverage, you should not. Alcohol reduces your ability to control what you say, and that is not something you want during an interview.

Interview Checklist
Take the following things to any interview:
- Copies of your resume. Although you have previously submitted, they get misplaced and it is not worth the time during the interview to look for them.
- A sheet of information to complete the application form that includes names, addresses, phone numbers for past jobs, dates of employment, names of past supervisors, information on your pay for jobs, plus information on your degrees and schools attended.
- A list of researched questions to ask.

You may discover halfway through the interview that you are not a good fit and you don't want the job. We suggest that you go forward and do your best anyway. Sometimes there are other unadvertised jobs that are better fits. Always keep your options open.

The real key to a successful interview is to know yourself and to know what you have to offer. If you have done all of your pre-work and planning, you should be able to help the interviewer understand what you can bring to their organization.

Using Search Firms, Headhunters, Temporary Agencies
If you are looking to make a confidential search, it may be a good idea to work with an executive search firm or headhunter. They can find jobs for you without revealing your name until the company is sure it wants to talk with you. Though some firms only deal with jobs that are in the six figures, there are some that place professionals at lower levels.

You should make sure that the firm has a good reputation and is effective by asking for references, etc. You need to control who your resume is sent to, and it is not unreasonable to ask the recruiter to check in with you in advance of forwarding it to a company, especially if your search is confidential. Being in Human Resources can be an advantage and a disadvantage here since it is a "small world" and you may have situations bordering on conflict of interest. On the other hand, your HR peers may know about good companies to work with. Remember, these firms are usually being paid by their client, so they are not necessarily working for your benefit. Some firms try to push candidates to take a job even if the person is not sure since they often get paid only when they fill the job. Some headhunters are job or industry specific. For example, there are firms that specialize in placing publishing professionals (including HR professionals) or that specialize in placing HR professionals in various industries.

In some states it is legal for career counselors to charge an individual to find a job for them. Before considering this route, make sure it is legal in your state and that they are legitimate businesses. If you are "in transition" between jobs, need income, and your search is taking a long time, you might consider working with a professional temporary or contract agency. Several of these agencies specialize in HR positions. Some companies who are looking for temporary contractors source for them directly, you would hear about them through word of mouth as you would for full-time opportunities. You are likely to earn more if you contract directly with the company because there is no intermediary to collect a fee. Many have temporary to permanent situations where companies try out people before taking them on as employees. The temporary work also demonstrates a willingness to work that makes your resume look better (as opposed to having a large gap in employment). But be careful that you don't take too much valuable search time working in a job with no potential.

Show Me the Money

We've mentioned that you should wait for the company to bring up the subject of money since you want to appear focused on the job and company. It is, however, a good idea to have some idea about what the job pays. You might want to ask about the general range before you go for an interview. Be prepared for the recruiter to ask you want kind of a range you are looking for. You should have some idea about what you can live with before answering this question. Reviewing your financial needs should be part of your pre-search prep work.

You may be willing to take a pay cut if you are looking at a job as a stepping stone into a company or as a means to gain experience in a particular industry or HR functional area. If you have been out of work for a while, you may be willing to take less to get some income. Though this can lead to questions later for future employers, if you think it through and don't stay too long in the lower paying job, it will not hurt your future plans. Be prepared to explain it though.

Researching the pay levels for various jobs can help you narrow the jobs you wish to apply for. The Internet is a good source of salary information, but be cautious of some of the "free" sites that offer this information, as the data may not be accurate. Most large job board sites have some kind of salary calculator you can use. Also, check out professional associations, as they often do salary studies that are available to members.

If you are willing to relocate, make sure you do some checking on the cost of living in other areas. What looks like a nice pay hike may not be so much if you are going from Pittsburgh to New York City, where the cost of living is much higher.

 Final Thoughts

- Don't get discouraged if you don't get the job you want right away.
- Be open to consider alternatives or side roads on your career path; they may lead to better opportunities.
- Be prepared by doing all your homework.
- Work at expressing confidence in yourself.
- Practice an "elevator" speech — a short description of who you are and what you are looking for, something that can be expressed in a trip in an elevator or on a brief phone call.

Moving Through Roadblocks

Sofia has been in Human Resources for about 10 years, and is currently a senior manager in the labor group of an aerospace company. Earlier in her career, she received several promotions and was satisfied with her ability to move up in the organization. However, recently her career advancement has fallen off. Also, she has seen several director-level, well-regarded females leave the organization to pursue higher-level jobs or start their own businesses. She is wondering what she can do to take her career to the next level.

Carmela and her family recently migrated to the United States from Chile, where she had some HR-related experience in a mining company. She would like to leverage this experience to start an HR job in a multi-national corporation.

Richard is a returning veteran from Afghanistan, where he had been deployed for three years, and where he received commendations for his ability to lead his troops. His military leave is about to end and he is expecting to return to the job he had for five years before he left in the HRIS division of a software manufacturing company. He has some anxiety about returning to the workforce after being gone for so long.

John has been working at his latest HR position for two years and has been with the company for seven years. He has completed an advanced degree in Human Resources and has had several promotions. Things were going well until recently when he got a new boss who seems to be looking for evidence that he's not doing a good job. He originally thought it was because they had different views on things but the boss mentioned something last week about John having a same-sex partner. He's concerned that his personal life is limiting his professional opportunities; something he never thought would happen in Human Resources.

No matter how well you plan your HR career trip, you are bound to encounter problems on the way. Sometimes there are barriers you face because of your gender, race, disability, or factors that you can't control. In this chapter, we will take a look at these issues and problems, and provide some strategies for dealing with them so that you can get back on track to your HR career success.

Brick Walls and Barriers

Much of the current business structure in the United States was developed by and led by white males. The success of business is a tribute to their leadership, but the world is changing. Current demographics tell us that in upcoming years this group will be a minority as more women enter the workforce and as our ethnic mix changes due to immigration and globalization.

The role of Human Resources is to set the company standard for being fair minded to all groups from a legal and ethical standpoint. Human Resources should carry the "diversity torch" by encouraging all groups to contribute the organization's success. Some HR departments strive to staff their group in a way that reflects the diversity patterns of their internal clients and external customers. Often, people are comfortable receiving services from those with whom they believe they have the most in common. Our HR role is to encourage inclusion because it is the best way any organization can take advantage of the best available talent to ensure future success.

However, it is not a perfect world, and if you are not part of the majority in your organization, you may experience barriers to your career growth. Glass ceilings and prejudices are realities. On the other hand, your "difference" may work to your advantage as companies strive to have more balanced teams that are representative of the community served by your organization. In the past, decision-makers were positioned to choose people with whom they were culturally compatible. The growing talent shortages in the workforce make every employee valuable regardless of their gender, race, religion, sexual preference, or any other factor. Admittedly, despite the best of intentions, some decision-makers are not equipped to understand the cultural differences that extend beyond their own ethnic group.

Our intent is *not* to stereotype issues of a particular gender or ethnic group. Since we are limited by the length of this book, we have included general observations.

To be successful, you may need to educate others about your diversity status so that they can appreciate your strengths and become aware of unreasonable prejudices that might be holding you back. Form alliances with others in your diverse group, and identify resources that specialize in your diverse group.

Gender Issues

Why Comment on the Gender?

While women today hold the majority of HR jobs and have successful careers in Human Resources, many hit the proverbial brick wall when they try to enter the realm of the C-Suite. After being unsuccessful in doing so, some become resigned to stay in their current role, while others become frustrated and leave the organization to start businesses of their own. Still others pursue careers outside of Human Resources and enter the senior level or C-Suite by transitioning to another functional group.

Though some of the following information is unique to recognized female strengths and strategies, the basic ideas are valid for men too.

Women's Strengths

Women have many of the aptitudes and skills to be successful in the HR profession. In *Emotional Intelligence*, the author's premise is that successful businesspersons are those who have mastered what are often referred to as the "soft" skills around harnessing relationships and interpersonal skills.[1] These are skills that women have championed historically. By understanding these "soft" skills and building on those that you possess, you have a good shot at advancing your career.[2]

What strengths do women have that put them in an excellent position to lead? Based on our experience working with and for many women in Human Resources, we believe the following:

- In today's flattened organizational structures, women are highly successful in working in matrixed organizations. They tend to be highly intuitive, able to quickly assess and mobilize human assets by assigning them to the appropriate role and drawing on their strengths.
- They are known to be adept at multi-tasking despite today's shrinking resources.

- Women mix well with a variety of leadership styles in the organization and can be role models for the growing representation of women in the workforce.
- They have firsthand understanding of the needs of their constituents around work-life balance, family leave, flexible scheduling, and other key issues in the workplace. In their roles at home with their families, they are affected by the constant need to juggle the needs of work and family.
- Women are in a position to make good judgments around strategy and policy affecting an employee's physical and mental well-being — based on their firsthand experience in their own lives working closely with their family and their community. They may have a "leg up" on the man who hasn't had this experience because his wife or significant other has traditionally handled the family and community issues in their relationship.

Career Progression for Women in Human Resources
Women in Human Resources have enjoyed long and satisfying careers. Compared to their colleagues in other functions, their retention rate in the business surpasses those in other functions. On the other hand, according to *The Athena Factor*,

> *52% of highly qualified women in these categories quit their jobs. Attrition rates spike ten years into their careers around age 35, when obstacles became more apparent and family pressures intensify.*"[3]

What Can Women Do to Advance Themselves?
Women in Human Resources need to articulate the bottom-line impact of the potential talent drain facing corporations. The Athena Factor study states: "the potential for change never has been greater because companies can no longer afford to lose half their female talent in an era of skilled labor shortages." While the talent leakage originates from other functional groups outside Human Resources, here are some strategies that women use to stay in the organization, garner career satisfaction, and advance:

Training and Education
- There are excellent programs on executive development, and many of them are offered on weekends. Find out how your scores and preferences on tests and assessments compare with the profile of C-Suite executives.

- Find your company's competencies for executive-level positions, assess how you measure up, and then pursue the education.

Assimilation in the Business
- Be prepared to volunteer for lateral career moves — or even demotions — to help add to your knowledge or experience base.
- Develop an excellent understanding of the business with particular attention to strategy, financial drivers, and budgets. These are roles typically dominated by men.
- Participate in meetings, events, and social gatherings that C-Suite executives attend. Understand their culture and how it works. Take up golf or other sports that are social outlets within men's groups.

Communication/Management Skills
- Ask for it! Initiate conversations with the appropriate person in your organization about your potential to advance. Express interest in advancement and find out how you are really viewed. Communicate goals and enlist the help of management to help eliminate the gaps.
- Develop behaviors that are more exemplary in executive ranks. Adjust your style to be more direct where appropriate, and be sure you drive results that impact the bottom line of the business.
- Take definite positions on issues in the workplace, and find some organizational "causes" with which you are connected.
- Think about your language — you may be unknowingly using vocabulary that does not position you as a strong leader.
- Learn how to negotiate for the things you want as opposed to simply giving things with no return.
- Learn how to leverage the differences to improve relationships and gain acceptance. The goal is not to transform into a male "look alike," but to enhance personal style by adopting the knowledge and skills practiced by successful males.
- Be a leader and role model for other women in your organization and in the community.

Internal Relationships
- Align with successful women who are members of the C-Suite. Engage these women as mentors to learn what they did to overcome the barriers that others face. Be sure to understand the personal commitment and impact of advancement to home and family life.

- Develop relationships with successful men who are members of the C-Suite who have a genuine interest in promoting the advancement of women in the workforce. Consider mentorships with successful men as well.
- Find other key executives in the workforce who will support women's goals. Let them know career goals and enlist their input.
- Find someone who will sponsor, market, and sell you to the decision-makers. This person may or may not be your mentor.

External Relationships

- Take steps to heighten your visibility in the community. Volunteer for board positions and fund-raising roles that can help you learn how to drive revenue for an organization.
- Attend company briefings when you can. Be active in these meetings by asking questions, making a point, and staying to discuss a point with a speaker. Join business organizations that are attended by business people at the executive level.
- Check the web and ask your networking contacts about women's networking events and support groups within your community.

Table 10.1 **Gender-Issues Plan**

Focus	Who Can Help?	Dates

Ethnic and Racial Minorities

Globalization, immigration, and other factors have caused the number of ethnic groups in our population to grow. This trend is expected to grow in the future. As of July 2005, the Census Bureau reports a total U.S. population of 296.4 million. Of this total, Hispanics comprise 42.7 million Americans while blacks — including both African Americans and more recently arrived Africans and blacks of Caribbean origin — total 39.7 million. The Census identified 14.4 million Asians, 4.5 million American Indians and Alaska natives, and nearly 1 million native Hawaiians and Pacific Islanders.

"These mid-decade numbers provide further evidence of the increasing diversity of our nation's population," said Census Bureau Director Louis Kincannon.[4]

The result will be that Caucasians will dwindle to minority status in the future. For this reason, regardless of your race or ethnic background, this section may apply to most people.

As a member of a minority ethnic group, you may encounter challenges to feeling accepted and feeling optimistic about growing your career. Sometimes these challenges may present themselves as forms of discrimination. However, we believe that most often, what you are experiencing is a lack of knowledge or understanding about your culture and ethnic group. There needs to be increased education on all sides. Most folks are likely to gravitate to those who are most like them because that is where they are most comfortable.

Work on those factors that are in your control to further your integration in the organization. Be proactive and educate others about your ethnic group to remove the element of mystery that some will perceive. If your cultural heritage requires you to do certain rituals during the day or to wear certain clothing, look on this as an opportunity to break down barriers. Here are some tips you might try:

Training and Education

- If your first language is not English and you plan to work in a U.S. company, make sure your language communications skills are as good as they can be. There are many sources for adults to get ESL (English as a Second Language) training. Courses are offered on a variety of skill levels.
- Become conversant on your company's current or planned global operations, which may be a source of future career opportunities for you.

Assimilation in the Business

- Start an affinity group at work for your ethnic group and demonstrate your leadership skills. Educate the workforce about the history and culture of your groups.
- Select mentors or coaches with your ethnicity or race in mind, but don't ignore those in mainstream groups

Internal Relationships

- Start a group to educate the workforce about the culture or language of your group; and sponsor a diversity day to showcase customs, dress, food, communication styles, and etiquette.
- If you work for an international company, volunteer for assignments or projects in geographies that would be supportive of your ethnic background.

External Relationships

- Look for organizations, associations, and community group web sites that relate to your ethnic group. Network with community leaders in these groups.
- Seek out recruiters, consulting groups, and web sites that specialize in jobs for your diverse group.
- Consider looking for companies that want to do business in an ethnic community or with an ethnic group you understand.
- Consider starting or joining a group on a social networking site or starting a community group.

Table 10.2 **Ethnic and Racial Minorities**

Focus	Who Can Help?	Dates

Military Veterans

At this writing, the United States is and has been engaged in several military conflicts across the world. As a result, many young people returning from active duty and military roles are entering and re-entering the workforce. They may be in the workforce for awhile and then be called out again for another tour of duty.

If you are part of this military group, your focus should be on communicating how your military experiences relate to U.S. jobs. However, as you return to the United States, you may be faced with a business environment that (a) has changed since you have been away or (b) doesn't understand your background or appreciate your education and experience. You probably have employment gaps on your resume due to your military service.

Here are some ideas for overcoming possible barriers:

Training and Education
- Ensure you are receiving all your benefits as a veteran.
- Be familiar with you rights under the Uniformed Services Employment and Reemployment Rights Act (USERRA).
- Look for transferability of skills (i.e., recruiting, managing, supervising troops) that are applicable anywhere, and learn to translate military titles into civilian terms.

Assimilation in the Business
- Look for opportunities to apply HR skills in military assignments and apply military experience to jobs at home when you return.
- Get up-to-speed on business developments (financial results, new product lines, changes in business strategy) in your company so you are able to relate when you return.
- Review your company's benefits and compensation package so you understand what you are entitled to as a returning civilian.
- Seek out others in the company who are in a similar situation.

Communication and Management Skills
- Start a blog or web site for those in similar situations to network/educate.
- Volunteer to write or speak about your experiences. An area of focus should be the leadership component of your military role as it has a generic application to many company jobs.

Internal Relationships
- Network with military career people in your company (or at other target companies where you might like to work) who are in leadership positions. Network with colleagues and counterparts in similar situations in trying to assimilate back into the workforce.

External Relationships
- Check out career services that help with repatriation.
- Look at companies that do business with the military as future employers.

Table 10.3 **Military Veterans**

Focus	Who Can Help?	Dates

People with Disabilities

This group consists of those who have a temporary disability and those who are permanently disabled in some way. Anyone may find themselves in this group at some point. Even if you don't have a disability now, you could have an accident or develop an age-related disability.

Depending on the situation, your disability can put a crimp in your career. In the case of a temporary disability, your career plans may need to go on the back burner for a period of time. However, sometimes a delay can work to your advantage as it may afford you additional time to make contacts or research your next move, gain additional perspective, and spend additional time with friends and family. If the disability occurs during a financial downturn, it gives you an opportunity to ride out the storm and pick up your plan when the economy improves. At any rate, you will certainly have a credible explanation for why you didn't move forward with your career for a period of time.

If your disability is permanent, you may have been living with it for a period of time and have had to make adjustments in other areas of your life to manage the situation. You probably have had experience in communicating your situation with those you encounter. The workplace is a different area, and you will want to consider how much you reveal about your situation to your manager and co-workers. While this is clearly a personal decision, you do want to give thought to how the information will be used, as well as to the potential career impact. Currently, the workplace is generally sensitive to exchanging medical information due to the Health Insurance Portability and Accountability Act (HIPAA) and other potential legal challenges.

Our advice on either temporary or personal disabilities is to reveal only information that relates to the performance of the job. For example, if you have to leave the office at 10 a.m. on a daily basis for physical therapy, you will need to communicate this to your manager. However, you could simply state that you need to leave to get some medical treatment. If you indicate it is for radiation, an assumption will be made that you have cancer, and things can snowball from there. While your situation may be treatable, you don't want people to infer that you are on your deathbed, especially when you are thinking about pursuing that next promotion once your treatment is completed.

Some folks derive great comfort from confiding in colleagues in the workplace. It is important to remember what your role is in the organization, the impact of sharing medical information, and the consequences that can follow.

Here are some tips that may help:

Training and Education
- Research and take advantage of government and social service programs for career assistance and accommodation information. The Job Accommodation Network (JAN) is a service provided by the U.S. Department of Labor's Office of Disability Employment Policy (ODEP). Its mission is to facilitate the employment and retention of workers with disabilities by providing employers, employment providers, people with disabilities, their family members, and other interested parties with information on job accommodations, entrepreneurship, and related subjects.[5]
- Focus on essential job functions which are used under protections in the federal Americans with Disabilities Act (ADA) and ADA Amendments Act (ADAAA), and develop your skill sets accordingly.
- Research people in the public arena with disabilities who became advocates and developed strong leadership abilities as a result. Evaluate how their accomplishments can be applied to your own situation.

Assimilation in the Business
- Teach people about your disability with the focus on what you *can* do. Most people are compassionate and sensitive once they understand your abilities.
- If you need help, offer suggestions for needed accommodations as specified in federal and state laws.

Internal Relationships

- Create an initiative around bringing people with abilities and disabilities on board; lead fund-raising and community events; and create a best practice for your company.
- Find people in leadership positions within your company with whom you can forge relationships. These people can help advocate your cause.

External Relationships

- If you need more costly accommodations, look to large companies, which are likely to have the resources available.
- Volunteer at a nonprofit group pertaining to your disability. This could lead to permanent employment at that group.

Table 10.4 **Disabilities**

Focus	Who Can Help?	Dates

Gay/Lesbian/Bisexual/Transgender (GLBT)

HR professionals need to advocate inclusive nondiscrimination policies and benefits for gay, lesbian, bisexual, and transgender (GLBT) employees and their families. According to the Human Rights Campaign Foundation, 90 percent of Fortune 500 companies include workplace protections for these groups, and more than half of Fortune 500 companies have same-sex partner benefits.[6] The need for recognition and inclusion is heightened by the war for talent and customers.

Companies have discovered that there is a huge market for products and services in the GLBT population and have made efforts to woo their business. Many companies have recognized the importance of this group to be properly represented in the workforce by expanding their benefits plans to cover registered domestic partners.

As with the other diversity groups discussed in this chapter, there is a need to improve understanding and reduce barriers about the GLBT population. Discretion is needed about what you tell people in the workplace about your sexual orientation. While some folks tend to be more private (allowing their colleagues to draw their own conclusions), others are more comfortable with full disclosure as they believe that not doing so can impede relationship-building. This is a personal decision and needs to be thought through along with the potential career implications. Many of the tips outlined for other groups in this chapter apply to the GLBT workforce.

Here are several that we believe are important:

- Check county, state, and municipal laws to verify the current state of anti-discrimination legislation about these groups.

- Assess your policy statements, handbooks, and other documents that mention diversity, and ensure they are updated to be in compliance with federal, state, and local laws. Include nondiscrimination statements about GLBT groups. You may want to consult with legal counsel to make sure the language passes muster.

- Assess the environment in your workplace relating to current or potential hostility or discrimination involving these groups. Develop a campaign to ensure these groups are treated with the same dignity and respect as any other group in the workplace. As part of your campaign, develop advocates and allies in the workplace who can help you build support and educate. Build relationships with key company officials who are known to have a similar lifestyle. They can be excellent mentors and coaches for you.

- Join an affinity group for socialization, education, and the opportunity to lead initiatives in this area.

- Take advantage of the services of your company's employee assistance program (EAP) to address any adjustment issues you are having or if you just need to talk to a trained professional. The same applies to assistance for any group discussed in this chapter.

Table 10.5 **Gay/Lesbian/Bisexual/Transgender (GLBT)**

Focus	Who Can Help?	Dates

Older Workers

With an aging workforce in most developed countries, issues surrounding older workers are becoming more prevalent. In a slow economy, older workers could face more unemployment as organizations look to lay off those workers who are more costly or who don't have up-to-date skills. Despite the protections of the federal Age Discrimination in Employment Act (ADEA) and state laws protecting individuals who are over 40 years old, companies do find ways to terminate older workers.

Economics may well drive people to want to work longer but they may be looking for more flexible schedules or even alternative career paths that focus on what they enjoy doing most in Human Resources. Consulting or teaching are two likely paths you might want to pursue if you have many years of HR experience and strong skills in HR practice. Both present potential part-time or flexible work arrangements. In addition, if companies need to cut costs but still maintain intellectual capacity, they may want to retain their older workers in coaching capacities to groom younger HR professionals.

The following are some things you can do to help yourself if you are an older worker who wants to continue to work.

- Keep your skills sharp and continue to take professional development courses whenever possible.
- Volunteer for assignments and task forces to demonstrate your interest and vitality.
- If your technical skills are rusty because you didn't grow up with a keyboard attached to your fingers, take some classes and practice. Often, HR executives have had administrative help and have not learned how to use technology; strong tech skills could be the difference between being retained or laid off.
- Search the Internet for information on aging and work, and join social networking groups that include all ages.
- Build your network so that it includes people of all ages.
- Work hard to stay fit, because aging has a greater impact if you are a smoker or overweight.
- Take advantage of the services of your company's EAP to address any adjustment issues you are having or if you just need to talk to a trained professional. The same applies to assistance for any group discussed in this chapter.

Table 10.6 **Older Workers**

Focus	Who Can Help?	Dates

 Final Thoughts

- It is likely that, at some point in your career, you will have to deal with challenges associated with one or more of the situations we have discussed in this chapter.
- It is a good reminder that the career route is not a straight line, but rather an evolution.
- The common thread of advice that we have given you for all these situations is to be your own advocate and proactively educate others to break down the barriers of misunderstanding.
- Doing so will build your self-confidence too, which will be necessary as you prepare for your next career move.
- You may not be able to educate or change an organization or situation to allow for your career progression.
- Sometimes, despite your best efforts, you should just quit trying and find a different route to move your career forward.

11
Career Derailment: What If the Train Falls Off the Tracks?

John was moving along with his career plans. After completing a Master's degree in HR it looked like he was on track to move into an assistant manager job of the company he had been recruited to join 3 years ago. Due to a major downturn in business, a month ago, the company merged with its largest competitor. A week later, John's boss met with him and told John his job was being eliminated. John was in total shock at first, and then he felt very betrayed and angry. Though he was usually very professional, he blew up at the meeting. "I'm really pis... off!" he yelled. "You recruited me from a secure position and told me I was on the fast track, now this!" The boss responded calmly, "Look, John, I know you are very upset right now. And you have a right to your feelings. But, you have a lot to offer the next company and if you carry your anger with you it will hurt you. No employer wants to hire someone who is dealing with anger over a past situation. Before you look for the next step in your career, you need to find ways to deal with your emotions." "How do you expect me to do that?" he said, still feeling upset. A few days later, John's boss's words came back to him and he started to look for help in dealing with his emotions and resources for getting his career back "on track."

It Can Happen to Anyone

Losing a job is something that we believe most business people experience once or more during their careers. This is not necessarily a reflection of you and often is something you have little or no control over. There are times when a small company is successful and the owner decides to sell to realize a return on his or her investment.

Business cycles, mergers and acquisitions, and economic pressure have an impact on headcount, and Human Resources is no exception. Many older workers struggle with losing a position that they thought would last to retirement. But surviving a job loss may actually make you look better. In the type of down economy that we are facing at this writing, resumes of candidates who haven't experienced restructuring and downsizing might be looked at skeptically. The thought is that those folks may have not taken tough positions; they may have not taken risks for fear of losing their jobs. Being downsized may be viewed as an inevitable part of being in business.

The bottom line is that you need to step back and regroup, and continue moving forward in your career rather than let the loss defeat you.

Types of Derailments

We have talked about circumstance over which you have little or no control that might result in barriers to your HR career progress. There are other circumstances that also present challenges — career-derailing events like layoffs, terminations, or changes in company structure (your "next career move" just disappeared due to a restructuring). Sometimes your career progress and plan depends on having a particular boss, but then that person leaves and the new boss is not as supportive of your "plans."

When you are moving at a good pace down the career road and suddenly it takes a turn you don't expect or you arrive at a dead end, it can be an emotional challenge. For many people, losing a job is statistically up there as a major life crisis on par with dealing with a death.

If you are dedicated to developing your career and at least a part of your self-identity is tied up in what you do, the blow of losing it can be devastating. It is first and most important to realize that the feelings you have related to job loss are perfectly normal.

As HR professionals, we are often part of the termination or layoff process, but that doesn't mean we can deal with our own situation. Many HR professionals may stay on board when a company closes and be the ones to "turn the lights off." Because of this responsibility of dealing with everyone else and keeping the spirits up to the end, we may not take the time to deal with our own feelings.

Deal with Your Feelings

Before you begin to get back on the road, it is vital that you recognize and deal with your feelings. Unresolved anger or fear will show when you try to find that next job, and it may increase your derailed time since no employer wants to hire a negative or distracted person, particularly in Human Resources. Our jobs are stressful enough without bringing lots of baggage along.

Consider the stages of grief so that you can work through these normal feelings. Keep in mind that everyone may not have all of these feelings and that not everyone may experience them in any particular order. Also, you may get past your anger, but it may come back. The stages modified for job loss are:[1]

1. Anger — that "dirty so-and-so"
2. Depression — like being in a pit: dark thinking, not wanting to start looking
3. Revenge — I'll get back at them, everyone will know that was not a good place to work
4. Vulnerability — my plans for the future are gone, my career plan is off course
5. Loneliness — "they" are at work and here I am at home
6. Self-doubts — I can't perform, I've failed
7. Embarrassment — how do my kids, spouse, family, friends, enemies view me?
8. Resignation — feeling sorry but accepting the situation
9. Resolution — I can come out of this, possibly for the better. I might find a better job
10. Rebound into action — Getting up and out, reforming the plan and taking action

Where to Start

Use the transition steps we covered in Chapter 10, but first you need to do some re-evaluation to find a new route, to repack your suitcase, and maybe even to determine a new destination.

Facing Realities

First, evaluate your financial situation realistically. Do a financial audit, including:

- Income sources, severance, unemployment compensation, vacation pay
- Savings, cash and investments, considering penalties if you use them

- Income from other family members or savings you could realize by tightening your budget
- Length of time before you need to bring in more money

The audit will help you determine how long you can focus on getting a job. It will also keep your choice of positions focused and make you less likely to take something just because of the money.

Second, it is a bad idea to "take a few months off" even if you were provided with a good severance package, and you don't need to work for the money. Unless you are at a point in your life where your career is a low priority in your value system, it does not impress a future employer if you take too much time off. It makes that new organization wonder if you want to or really need to work.

This might be a good time to go back to school and become a full-time student to get that advanced degree in Human Resources. Education demonstrates a commitment to your professional development. For those who just lost a job, spending money on education may be unrealistic. You may want to consider any skill or knowledge building programs, even if they are not directly related to Human Resources. It's worth looking into scholarships, low-cost programs, webinars, or your local unemployment office programs.

If you do decide to return to school, it is important to know what that education will do for your career and how soon. If you are counting on education to take you to a new career, be sure to do the research to verify that this is the case as well as whether there is a need in the marketplace for the career you aspire to. While there are no guarantees, school is both time-consuming and expensive. You want to be reasonably sure there is a payback.

Third, get the support of your family and friends. You need to concentrate on the work of getting a job. It is not unusual for others to assume that now you have more time on your hands and they may come to expect you to help with other things. You need to meet with them and discuss the importance of what you are doing. If you have been in Human Resources for any length of time, they are probably used to some long or irregular hours, so just let them know that nothing has changed.

Asking for help is difficult for some of us. As HR professionals, we are usually the ones helping others or being in charge of the career planning. Finding yourself in a situation you didn't have any control over may tempt you not to talk about it. But if you don't get others on board to help, the detour will last longer.

Getting cooperation and help from family and friends will reduce your stress and allow you to focus on the task of looking for a job.

Why the Detour?

If your career detour has occurred because of a change in the industry or the market you find yourself in, you may need to go back to basics and re-evaluate your chances of reaching your original destination. You may need to take a job in another industry or consider relocation if you want to stay in Human Resources.

One example is an HR professional we spoke to who was growing her career in the dot-com field. She moved up quickly as the industry grew and she became an expert in the culture found in the creative, highly technical employee base of that industry. When the "bust" occurred, she suddenly found herself without a job. To make matters worse, when she applied for jobs in different industries, she was not taken seriously since she had no other industry experience. In addition, the California Silicon Valley had serious unemployment issues. She took a lower-level job in another industry to ensure continuing income, went back to school to get an advanced degree and sat for her SPHR certification. The result, a few years later, was a move to a higher-level job in her new company.

Ask for Help from the Former Employer

Unless you were terminated for cause, it is always a good idea to see what you can negotiate as far as help is concerned. Many companies are willing to provide some recommendations, outplacement services, or other help.

It is also OK to ask for severance or benefits continuation. Check to see if the company has a policy related to severance payments. Severance is usually based on years of service, but even if you have not been with the company for long they may be willing to provide something to keep the exit on a positive note. If they provide any help, you will likely be asked to sign a separation agreement that includes specific language about what you are getting and requires you to keep the details confidential. You should have an attorney review any document you sign.

As an HR professional, you may know what the company has done for individuals in the past. It gives you the opportunity to ask for help for yourself. Remember, they can only say "no," so you have nothing to lose. It is very important to maintain professional demeanor and composure when you are negotiating. The company wants to preserve its reputation — as do you. In addition, you don't want to burn any bridges with individuals whom you may need as business contacts in the future.

Talk to other managers in the organization whom you've worked with and ask for their help, support, and network contacts. Even if the company has a "no references" policy, sometimes people can still help with leads or are free to respond from a personal perspective vs. as a representative of the company.

What If You Got Fired?

Though in Human Resources we usually try to avoid hiring someone who got fired, we all recognize that even the best of us make mistakes at times. If you got fired for any reason, you need to work through what might be strong emotions first. Then you need to find a credible way to explain the termination.

We suggest you talk to a trusted advisor, and, if needed, legal counsel, so you can ensure that all of your rights are protected. Consider developing a reference statement with your supervisor before you leave so you know how references will be handled. We have talked to people who even prepared a reference and asked management to edit it until both were comfortable with the language. Talk about the possibility of getting references from other company managers or clients outside of Human Resources.

Terminations can occur because of a disagreement on policy, a mistake you made, or even because of a personality clash with your boss or co-workers. If your recent employer is likely to state that you were terminated, you want to be able to address the reasons in nonemotional terms without complaining or whining about it. If the termination was because of a mistake you made, you *must* be able to explain what happened and what you learned from the experience.

Get Down to Work

As we said before, it is important to get started with the job search quickly. Having work to do will help you keep in the work mode and will increase your chances of finding something quicker. You may need to supplement your income by doing some temporary or part-time HR work while you look.

No matter the circumstances of your job loss, it is important *not* to complain about the former employer. That is why it is critical that you work through your emotional issues before you talk to a new employer. You need to be rational, factual, and comfortable with what you are saying.

Consulting

Consider doing some HR consulting work by using your networks to find tasks that larger HR departments want to outsource. Not only do you stay fresh in using your skills, but you also build credibility in the HR field. This work can even be on a volunteer basis, where you help a nonprofit with services they can't afford to pay for, such as creating job descriptions, an employee handbook, or developing employee policies. If paid, the work can be used to supplement your income while you look for a job within an organization. In addition, you may decide that you like consulting and may decide to put down roots there.

There are some larger organizations that provide services to HR departments such as outplacement firms. If the business climate is slow (possibly the reason why you lost your job), they may need some contract help. Helping others to find jobs can help you since they may be likely to remember you in their new company if an HR job becomes available.

Teaching

Teaching Human Resources or other business courses for a local college is also worth considering. Teaching helps you hone your presentation skills, update your own knowledge, and it exposes you to other HR professionals or business professionals who may be good networks for your job search. Get in touch with local colleges that offer courses you have the education and knowledge to teach, contact the dean to set an exploratory meeting, and talk to educators about how they got their work. Use the Internet to research schools. As with consulting, you may decide that the academic life is one you want to pursue.

Professional Temp HR

Finally, there are some professional temporary employment agencies that specialize in professional business and HR jobs. These temporary placement jobs give you some income, grow your reputation and networks, and demonstrate to a perspective employer that you are serious about working. They can allow you to explore different HR specialties or industries to plan you next career moves.

One caution about working while searching for a job is that if you use all of your time working at a job with no career potential, you will not have time to look for that next "real" job. But, sometimes, financial demands take precedence.

Get Back to the Real Plan as Soon as Possible

As you begin to do the things we suggested in Chapter 3, you should also reassess your plan for your career by asking yourself the following questions:

- Is my original career goal still reasonable?
- Is it reasonable to try and follow the same steps to move forward or do I take a permanent or temporary detour?
- What does my new map look like?
- Do I need to get other experience or education?
- What new contacts and networks do I need to develop to move forward?

What If I'm in the Same Job but My Boss Changed or My Mentor Is Gone?

Sometimes we get sidetracked in our HR career journey because the boss who was so supportive gets a new job, leaves, or gets fired or promoted. Maybe the new boss is not one to encourage his or her employees to develop their careers.

Consider if this is the best time to leave. How will your resume look if you change jobs now? What is the job market like for your job title in your geography? What is current state of business in the companies or industries you would target? How difficult has it been for those who have left your organization lately to land new jobs? You may decide to take your time and prepare before making a change.

You Have Several Options

The first option might be to give the situation time — the new boss may change his or her mind about supporting career development, or the new boss may leave.

Follow them to a new organization, if possible. But make sure that the opportunities are right for you. One HR professional who talked to us told of following one mentor to a company where she did get good experience in a new industry and in a company where they developed and valued their HR managers. The boss then heard of a job at a third company and advised her to go for it since it would help her advance her career. Later in her career journey, the same boss hired her back in a fourth company and all the while she kept going forward and moving up.

Establish a good working relationship with the new boss. This doesn't always work, but if you approach the individual in a positive way and get the working relationship started first, you may have a chance to have a new advocate. The new boss may have a need to retain you because of the history and knowledge you have about the company. Try to build on this value to get the relationship going. Ask him or her how you can help them. The chances of this happening in Human Resources may be better than other fields since a good HR professional is a competent coach.

You may be able to find a new mentor.

You may be best served to look outside the organization. The good news here is that you have time to re-evaluate and plan.

Before looking to leave, make sure you consider all the factors. It is usually a bad idea to "gut react" when you are disappointed about your boss' exit. Remember that the new boss may just be getting their feet wet and trying to establish their position, so try not to judge too harshly or quickly.

Career Derailment Can Be an Opportunity

Though we often look at changes that we didn't initiate as negative, sometimes a derailment can lead to a better direction for your career.

When her company was facing major change due to deregulation in the power industries in the 1990s, one HR manager we spoke with took a job in a manufacturing company. That position eventually led to a higher-level position in another manufacturing company that is a supplier to the power industry. Her current job is in a larger, growing company, where she has moved up to vice president of Human Resources. If not for the change in the industry more than 15 years ago, she might not have gained the manufacturing experience which she was able to combine with the power-industry experience to get to a higher level today.

It is important to look at derailments as opportunities to go for something better. Once you work through the disappointment, you might just find that the change was the best thing that could happen to you.

Another HR manager had been looking toward establishing her own consulting firm someday. She thought of this path as a way to work toward retirement as she did consulting and looked for some teaching assignments. With financial issues facing her manufacturing company and the possibility of her job going away, she accelerated her plans and after five years as a consultant says she's happy with her work helping small- and mid-sized companies solve their HR problems. Even now, facing a recessional economy, her business is probably established enough that she will survive. If she had waited several years to start, she might be facing a much different, tougher future.

 Final Thoughts

- Change in our career plans can be disruptive, but we need to be able to adjust if we want to get ahead in the long run.
- Work on getting over the emotional hills, then revise and work your way forward.
- Select a slightly (or totally) different direction with your career travel plan.
- Use the job search strategies outlined in Chapter 9.
- Keep in mind that derailment isn't just losing a job but also losing the opportunity for following the map you have plotted out — but it doesn't have to result in being stuck at a dead end.

Bon Voyage

The task of developing your HR career may always be an uphill climb. The good news is that Human Resources is now recognized by many as an important contributor in the success of most organizations. The meaningful work that Human Resources has done places us in greater demand, which presents more career opportunities both in HR roles and in line business roles. HR professionals are busier than ever as we work to keep on top of a rapidly changing business and legal environment. Not only do we need to keep up with developments within the business, but we also need to be knowledgeable about the factors that impact the people who make up our organizations — the human factor.

Meeting the challenge of being pulled in many directions and serving the needs of many "clients" may mean little time left over for ourselves. This was the key motivator for us in writing this book. We need to carve out appropriate time for our own career development on a consistent basis for the benefit of ourselves and the clients we serve.

It is most important then, that we take advantage of the resources and networks available to us. Today's technology can help us research effectively, reach out to our peers and experts quickly, and communicate efficiently. The Internet has made information available 24/7.

This book was written to provide you with some survival skills, tools, and techniques that will assist you on your career journey. We certainly don't have all of the answers, but our hope is that by sharing travel stories of ourselves and others we can motivate you to take control of your own career trip. We also hope that the ideas presented here will spark new and creative approaches that you will share with others in Human Resources.

The skills of career development shared here are targeted to our HR field, but many of the ideas can be used as you guide the careers of others.

As you embark on your career journey, you will find shortcuts and road-blocks. You will find helpful "travel agents" among your HR peers and professional colleagues. You will also find individuals and organizations that can't or won't help your progress. We are certain of all of these things. We are just as certain that if you are dedicated to investing time and planning in your travel arrangements, you will succeed.

You may find yourselves in places that you never pictured when you started on your career. With an open mind, the willingness to be a lifelong learner, and a belief in your own strengths, you will have a satisfying and exciting journey.

Human Resources Management is a wonderful, changing, and exciting (although at times frustrating) career path, but you will never be without a challenge!

Your future is in your hands. We encourage you to never give up on your-self, for only by investing in your own satisfaction will you be able to provide good service to others.

We wish you safe and satisfying travels. Bon Voyage!

Appendix

Instructions for Completing the HR Travel Itinerary

The template is organized into five sections: Goal Setting, Contacts, SHRM, Self-Assessment, and Skills with an additional section for observable results.

Goal Setting: You indicate what you want to accomplish both in a 12-month and a 3-year period, along with identifying contacts that can help.

Contacts: You know that you need a broader range of people in your professional life who can help you with goal attainment. Meeting them is generally the most challenging part. Networking is a key skill that HR professionals need to master. The practice of targeting people who can introduce you to other people who can help with your professional goals is the key. See Chapter 8 for more on networking.

SHRM: There are many resources available to members of professional associations, including courses, web sites, conferences, chapter meetings, and contacts that can be leveraged.

Self-Assessment: This is a place to summarize the introspective work done previously around life goals, job satisfiers, dissatisfiers, and how gaps will be addressed.

Skills: After reviewing performance appraisals, competency assessments, and other feedback mechanisms, this is a place to document skills to be leveraged and those needing improvement. It also includes a commitment to a mentor. (See Chapter 7 to see more on mentorships.)

Observable Results: This is probably the most important section of the template because committing to the results you want to see (and when) will further cement a commitment on your part and will provide for reinforcement when it happens. As with any goal-setting process, you want to indicate results that are observable, realistic, and quantifiable. It may be as simple as developing five contacts in a particular subject-matter expertise within a certain time period. Another example is beginning a mentor relationship with someone you are comfortable with in a given time period.

The "RX" can be customized to fit your own needs. It can be a tool to refer to regularly and will be revised as needed. By having your plans documented, it increases the commitment level on your part. Having a "witness" signing off on the plan with you will also provide a greater level of discipline that is needed to make your planning process successful.

HR Travel Itinerary

Goal Setting	12-Month Goal	3-Year Goal	5 key people I know who can help:	5 key people I'd like to know:
	☐ Change Jobs	Relocation: ☐ Yes ☐ No		
	☐ Lateral/Demotion	Industry		
	☐ Promotion	Role		
	☐ Leave Current Employer			
	☐ Status Quo			
Contacts	Current/Prior Bosses	Community Contacts/ Professional Contacts	Alma Mater Resources/ Career Center	Plan to Meet Them:
	Resources: ☐ Yes ☐ No			
	Who?			
SHRM	SHRM— Help/Contacts	HR Certification Institute/ Local and State Chapter Opportunities/National Opportunities	SHRM Helpful Websites	SHRM Conferences/Dates

continued on next page

HR Travel Itinerary (continued)

Self-Assessment	Life Priority	Job Satisfier	Job Dissatisfiers	Plan to fix?/Who can help?
	More:			
	Less:			
	Insight:			

Skills	Review/Insights	Skills needing improvement	Skills to leverage	Mentor Plan
	Performance Review			Stay the Course
	360-Degree Feedbacks			Get One
	Hogan			Replace
	Other Assessments			Steps Needed

Other Actions Planned:

Observable results within 6 months so I feel satisfied:

Date to revisit plan:

Plan:

Signed: _____ Date: _____ "Witness": _____ Date: _____

# Endnotes

Chapter 1

[1] Mike D'Ambrose, "Best Resolutions for a Great HR Career in 2008!" HR Journeys, Martha Finney, ed., Sunday, January 6, 2008. Accessible at http://hrjourneys.blogspot.com/2008/01/best-resolutions-for-great-hr-career-in.html.

[2] Matthew D. Breitfelder and Daisy Wademan Dowling, "Why Did We Ever Go Into HR?" *Harvard Business Review*, July-August 2008. Accessible, in part, at http://hbr.harvardbusiness.org/2008/07/why-did-we-ever-go-into-hr/ar/1.

Chapter 2

[1] Matthew D. Breitfelder and Daisy Wademan Dowling, "Why Did We Ever Go Into HR?" *Harvard Business Review*, July-August 2008. Accessible, in part, at http://hbr.harvardbusiness.org/2008/07/why-did-we-ever-go-into-hr/ar/1.

[2] Ed Frauenheim, "Going From CEO to HR Minder at Kohl's," *Workforce Management*, August 28, 2008. Accessible at http://www.workforce.com/section/00/article/25/73/61.php.

[3] Keith H. Hammonds, "Why We Hate HR," *Fast Company*, September 11, 2008. Accessible at http://www.fastcompany.com/magazine/97/open_hr.html?page=0%2C0.

[4] Ibid.

[5] Keith H. Hammonds, "How To Do HR Right," *Fast Company*, September 11, 2008. Accessible at http://www.fastcompany.com/magazine/97/open_hr-fasttake.html

Chapter 3

[1] "SHRM 2008 Managing Your HR Career," page 18, Society for Human Resource Management, February 2008.

[2] Adrienne Fox, "Corporate Social Responsibility Pays Off," *HR Magazine*, Vol. 52, No. 8, August 2007.

[3] "Are They Really Ready To Work? Employers' Perspectives on the Basic Knowledge and Applied Skills of New Entrants to the 21st Century U.S. Workforce," Conference Board, Corporate Voices for Working Families, the Partnership for 21st Century Skills, and the Society for Human Resource Management, 2006.

[4] "Changing Strategies in HR Technology and Outsourcing: 2007 HR Technology Trends Survey," Watson Wyatt World Wide Research Reports, 2007.

[5] Hannah Clark, "The fastest-growing jobs in the U.S.," *Forbes Magazine*, March 12, 2007.

Chapter 4

[1] "SHRM 2008 Managing Your HR Career," Society for Human Resource Management, February 2008.

[2] Susan M. Healthfield, "So You Think You Want a Career in Human Resources," About.com: Human Resources, 2008. Accessible at http://humanresources.about.com/od/hrbasicsfaq/tp/careers_in_hr.htm.

[3] "SHRM 2008 Managing Your HR Career," p. 21.

Chapter 5

[1] Leslie A. Weatherly "Competency Models Series Part I: Competency Models—An Overview," SHRM Research Department, Society for Human Resource Management, February 1, 2005.

[2] Jim Collins, *Good to Great: Why Some Companies Make the Leap* (New York: HarperBusiness, 2001).

[3] Kerry Patterson, et al., *Crucial Conversations: Tools for Resolving Broken Promises, Violated Expectations, and Bad Behavior* (New York: McGraw-Hill, 2005).

Chapter 6

[1] Karen Berman, et al., *Financial Intelligence for HR Professionals: What You Really Need to Know about Numbers* (Boston, Harvard Business School Press, 2008).

[2] G. Richard Shell and Marie Moussa, *The Art of Woo: Using Strategic Persuasion to Sell Your Ideas* (New York: Portfolio, 2007).

Chapter 7

[1] "Coaching and Mentoring: What's the Difference?" Brefi Group Limited: Birmingham, London, UK & International, 2009. Accessible at http://www.brefigroup.co.uk/coaching/coaching_and_mentoring.html.

[2] Chris Posti, Posti Associates, Interview 2008. Accessible at http://www.postiinc.com.

[3] *Webster's New World Dictionary and Thesaurus* (Hoboken, NJ: John Wiley and Sons, 2002).

[4] Erin Abrams, "Mentor Stories: My Personal Board of Directors," The Glass Hammer, March 24, 2008. Accessible at http://www.theglasshammer.com/news/2008/03/24/mentor-stories-my-personal-board-of-directors/.

[5] Jeffery Howard, "Exploring The MasterMind." Accessible at http://www.selfgrowth.com/articles/Exploring_The_MasterMind.html.

Chapter 8

[1] "The Changing Face at the Top," IMD International Search and Consulting, June 5, 2008.

[2] Ibid.

[3] Erin Binney, "HR Certification Pays Off in Satisfaction, if Not Dollars," SHRM Online, June 18, 2008. Accessible at http://www.shrm.org/about/news/Pages/HRCertificationPaysOff.aspx.

[4] James A. Hazen, Applied Behavioral Insights, Interview 2008. Accessible at http://www.appliedbehavioralinsights.com/index.html.

5 "HR Curriculum Guidebook & Template for Undergraduate and Gradu-
    ate Programs," Society for Human Resource Management, December
    1, 2005. Accessible at http://www.shrm.org/Research/SurveyFindings/
    Articles/Pages/SHRMHRCurriculumGuidebookTemplateforUndergradu-
    ateandGraduatePrograms.aspx.

Chapter 9
1 "SHRM 2008 Managing Your HR Career," Society for Human Resource
    Management, February 2008.
2 Ellen Sautter and Diane Crompton, "Seven Days to Online Networking," JIST
    Works, May 2008.

Chapter 10
1 Daniel Goleman, *Emotional Intelligence: Why It Can Matter More Than IQ*,
    10th Anniversary Edition (New York: Bantam, 2006).
2 Linda Babcock and Sara Laschever, *Women Don't Ask: Negotiation and the
    Gender Divide* (Princeton, NJ: Princeton University Press, 2003).
3 W. Michael Gear, *The Athena Factor* (New York: Forge, 2005).
4 "Nation's Population One-Third Minority," U.S. Census Bureau, CB06-72,
    May 10, 2006. Accessible at http://www.census.gov/Press-Release/www/
    releases/archives/population/006808.html.
5 Job Accommodation Network, http://www.jan.wvu.edu.
6 Human Rights Campaign Foundation, "The State of the Workplace for Gay,
    Lesbian, Bisexual and Transgender Americans" 2006-2007. Accessible at
    http://www.hrc.org/documents/State_of_the_Workplace.pdf.

Chapter 11
1 Elisabeth Kübler-Ross and David Kessler, *On Grief and Grieving: Finding the
    Meaning of Grief Through the Five Stages of Loss* (New York: Scribner,
    2005).

Additional Resources

Certification Sources

Benefits Management certification, Certified Benefits Professional (CBP), World at Work Society of Certified Professionals, www.worldatworksociety.org.

Compensation Strategy and Management certification, Certified Compensation Professional (CCP), World at Work Society of Certified Professionals, www.worldatworksociety.org.

Generalist HR Management certification, Professional in Human Resources (PHR), HR Certification Institute, www.hrci.org.

Generalist in Human Resources with specific world-wide business application certification, Global Professional in Human Resource Management, HR Certification Institute, www.hrci.org.

Labor Relations Professional Certification, HR Policy Association, www.hrpolicy.org.

Public Sector HR Certification, IPMA-Certified Professional (IPMA-CP) and IPMA-Certified Specialist (IPMA-CS); International Public Management Association for Human Resources (IPMA-HR), www.ipma-hr.org.

Senior-Level HR Generalist certification, Senior Professional in Human Resource Management, HR Certification Institute, www.hrci.org.

Total Rewards with a Global focus certification, Global Remuneration Professional (GRP), World at Work Society of Certified Professionals, www.worldatworksociety.org.

Work Life/Health and Wellness/Organizational Culture, Work-Life Certified Professional (WLCP), World at Work Society of Certified Professionals, www.worldatworksociety.org.

Books

Babcock, Linda and Sara Laschever, *Women Don't Ask: Negotiation and the Gender Divide* (Princeton, NJ: Princeton University Press, 2003).

Berman, Karen, et al *Financial Intelligence for HR Professionals: What You Really Need to Know About Numbers* (Boston, Harvard Business School Press, 2008).

Bliss, Wendy, *Essentials of Negotiation* (Boston: Harvard Business School Press, 2005).

Collins, Jim, *Good to Great: Why Some Companies Make the Leap — And Others Don't* (New York: Harper Business, 2001).

Gear, W. Michael, *The Athena Factor* (New York: Forge, 2005).

Goleman, Daniel, *Emotional Intelligence: Why It Can Matter More Than IQ*, 10th Anniversary Edition (New York: Bantam, 2006).

Kübler-Ross, Elisabeth and David Kessler, *On Grief and Grieving: Finding the Meaning of Grief Through the Five Stages of Loss* (New York: Scribner, 2005).

Losey, Mike et al (eds.), *The Future of Human Resource Management: 64 Thought Leaders Explore the Critical HR Issues of Today and Tomorrow* (Hoboken, NJ: John Wiley & Sons, 2005).

Palmer, Jeanne and Martha I. Finney, *The Human Resource Professional's Career Guide: Building a Position of Strength* (San Francisco: Pfeiffer, 2004).

Patterson, Kerry et al, *Crucial Conversations: Tools for Resolving Broken Promises, Violated Expectations, and Bad Behavior* (New York: McGraw-Hill, 2005).

Patterson, Kerry et al, *Influencer: The Power to Change Anything* (New York: McGraw-Hill, 2008).

Shell, G. Richard and Marie Moussa, *The Art of Woo: Using Strategic Persuasion to Sell Your Ideas* (New York: Portfolio, 2007).

Society for Human Resource Management, *Weathering Storms: Human Resources in Difficult Times* (Alexandria, VA: Society for Human Resource Management, 2008).

Sokolosky, Valerie, *Monday Morning Leadership for Women* (Dallas: CornerStone Leadership Institute, 2003).

Strayer, Susan D., *Vault Guide to Human Resources Careers* (New York: Vault, 2005).

Ulrich, Dave et al, *HR Competencies: Mastery at the Intersection of People and Business* (Alexandria, VA: Society for Human Resource Management, 2008).

Articles

Mike D'Ambrose, "Best Resolutions for a Great HR Career in 2008!" *HR Journeys*, Martha Finney, ed., Sunday, January 6, 2008. http://hrjourneys. blogspot.com/2008/01/best-resolutions-for-great-hr-career-in.html.

Matthew D. Breitfelder and Daisy Wademan Dowling, "Why Did We Ever Go Into HR?" *Harvard Business Review*, July-August 2008. Accessible, in part, at http://hbr.harvardbusiness.org/2008/07/why-did-we-ever-go-into-hr/ar/1.

Ed Frauenheim, "Going From CEO to HR Minder at Kohl's," *Workforce Management*, August 28, 2008. http://www.workforce.com/section/00/article/25/73/61.php.

Keith H. Hammonds, "Why We Hate HR," *Fast Company*, September 11, 2008. http://www.fastcompany.com/magazine/97/open_hr.html?page=0%2C0.

Keith H. Hammonds, "How To Do HR Right," *Fast Company*, September 11, 2008. http://www.fastcompany.com/magazine/97/open_hr-fasttake.html.

Adrienne Fox, "Corporate Social Responsibility Pays Off," *HR Magazine*, Vol. 52, No. 8, August 2, 2007.

Hannah Clark, "The fastest-growing jobs in the U.S.," *Forbes Magazine*, March 12, 2007.

Susan M. Healthfield, "So You Think You Want a Career in Human Resources," About.com: Human Resources, a part of the New York Times Company, 2008. http://humanresources.about.com/od/hrbasicsfaq/tp/careers_in_hr.htm.

"Coaching and mentoring – what's the difference?" Brefi Group Limited: Birmingham, London, UK & International, 2009. http://www.brefigroup.co.uk/coaching/coaching and mentoring.html.

Erin Abrams, "Mentor Stories: My Personal Board of Directors," *The Glass Hammer*, March 24, 2008. http://www.theglasshammer.com/news/2008/03/24/mentor-stories-my-personal-board-of-directors/.

"The Changing Face at the Top," IMD International Search and Consulting, June 5, 2008.

Erin Binney, "HR Certification Pays Off in Satisfaction, if Not Dollars," SHRM Online, June 18, 2008. http://moss07.shrm.org/about/news/Pages/HRCertificationPaysOff.aspx.

Ellen Sautter and Diane Crompton, "Seven Days to Online Networking," JIST Works, May 2008.

"Nation's Population One-Third Minority," U.S. Census Bureau, May 10, 2006.

"Strategic Leadership Development — A View From the Top," SHRM Research Translations, October 1, 2004.

Barbara Rose, "Workplace full of gender time warps," *Chicago Tribune*, June 5, 2008.

Web Sites

American Society for Training & Development, www.ASTD.org.

Assessment Center, www.appliedbehavioralinsights.com/index.html.

Bureau of Labor Statistics, www.bls.gov.

Coaching web site, www.postiinc.com.

Free business cards, www.vistaprint.com.

Job Accommodation Network, www.jan.wvu.edu.

The MasterMind, www.selfgrowth.com/articles/Exploring_The_MasterMind.html.

Society for Human Resource Management, www.SHRM.org.

Other

The HR Certification Institute has established detailed list of the Bodies of HR Knowledge that describe more on the various HR Specialty areas. Check out http://www.hrci.org/certification/bok/nbok/.

"SHRM 2008 Managing Your HR Career," page 18, Society for Human Resource Management, February, 2008.

"Are They Really Ready To Work?, Employers' Perspectives on the Basic Knowledge and Applied Skills of New Entrants to the 21st Century U.S. Workforce," Conference Board, Corporate Voices for Working Families, the Partnership for 21st Century Skills, and the Society for Human Resource Management, 2006.

"Changing Strategies in HR Technology and Outsourcing - 2007 HR Technology Trends Survey," Watson Wyatt World Wide Research Reports, 2007.

Leslie A. Weatherly "Competency Models Series Part I: Competency Models - An Overview," SHRM Research Department, Society for Human Resource Management, February 1, 2005.

HR Curriculum Guidebook & Template for Undergraduate and Graduate Programs, Society for Human Resource Management, December 1, 2005. shrm.org/Research/SurveyFindings/Articles/Pages/SHRMHRCurriculum GuidebookTemplateforUndergraduateandGraduatePrograms.aspx.

"The State of the Workplace for Gay, Lesbian, Bisexual and Transgender Americans," the Human Rights Campaign Foundation, 2006.

Rebecca R. Hastings, SPHR, "SHRM 2007 State of Workplace Diversity Management Report: A Call to Action," February 26, 2008.

INDEX

(Page numbers in *italics* indicate figurative, tabulated, or checklist materials.)

About the Authors

Nancy E. Glube has a 20 plus year career in Human Resources, currently as VP Business Solutions for Dale Carnegie of Georgia. Nancy's background includes leadership HR positions in a variety of industries, including Executive Director, HR for 13 years at Cingular Wireless (AT&T) Mobility as well as work in health care, international shipping and transportation, and consumer goods manufacturing. She has the versatility to excel in small, medium and large organizations. She also has experience as an HR consultant.

Nancy's focus has been translating HR strategy into winning business results. Functional areas of strength include: leadership development, talent assessment, mentoring, employee engagement, and retention. She has strong experience delivering HR services to large and diversified client bases. Also, she has an excellent track record developing high-performing HR teams.

Nancy is a speaker at previous SHRM conferences, and she has also been a member of several SHRM Special Expertise Panels. She is also actively taking interviews and fielding media questions for SHRM.

One of Nancy's areas of specialization includes the grooming and development of HR practitioners. A program she developed at AT&T has been adopted company-wide. She presented at the 2008 national convention on the topic of "Spa Treatment for Your HR Career."

Nancy holds both bachelor's and master's degrees from Binghamton University. She graduated from a study abroad program in Salamanca, Spain, and has knowledge of Spanish. Nancy's first career was in education, where she taught in secondary schools.

Phyllis G. Hartman, SPHR, is the founder of PGHR Consulting, Inc., and has nearly two dozen years of experience as an HR professional. A frequent speaker on career development, workforce development, and other HR and business topics, Phyllis was a member of SHRM's Employee Relations Panel for three years and the SHRM Workforce Readiness Committee for five years, and served as Chair in 2003. She has delivered programs at the SHRM Annual Conference (2007 — "Where Will They Come From: Creating a Business Case for Workforce Readiness Involvement in Your Organization"); as well as programs for the PA SHRM State Council, the Vermont and Virginia state councils, SHRM Student Conferences, and local chapters and other organizations. She was the Pennsylvania SHRM State Council Workforce Readiness Director 2005-2006.

In her business, Phyllis provides a variety of HR consulting services, including recruitment, outplacement coaching, employee relations consulting, and training to a wide variety of small- and mid-sized organizations. Prior to founding PGHR, she worked as a practitioner in HR management in for-profit manufacturing and nonprofit service sectors.

Phyllis holds a master's in Human Resource Management from La Roche College and a bachelor's in Education from Edinboro University of Pennsylvania. She is a certified Senior Professional in HR. She has been active with the Pittsburgh HR Association, serving numerous terms on the board of directors, including as president in 1997. Phyllis has written articles, white papers, and book chapters on HR topics, and teaches Human Resources and business courses at several Pittsburgh colleges and universities.

Phyllis lives outside Pittsburgh with her husband, Chuck. She is an active hiker, birdwatcher, and reader.